Historic Virginia Inns

A Cook's Tour

by
M'Layne Murphy

with
Jill Ungerman
and
Jerry Price

Photography
by
Kelly Harris

Cardinal Productions Inc.
Dallas, Texas

To Andrew and Meaghen Murphy

First printing October 1986
Second printing May 1987

Cardinal Productions, Inc.
Dallas, Texas 75219
© 1986 by Cardinal Productions, Inc.   All rights reserved.
ISBN 0-939245-00-0
Library of Congress Catalog Card Number 86-71909
Printed in the United States of America

Contents

Preface

You might say that the spirit of Thomas Jefferson, which lives on in Virginia, prompted me to write this book. As a gracious host, a gourmet of the highest degree, and a connoisseur of wines, he was extremely popular with friends who visited Monticello after his second term as President of the United States. Monticello became an inn of sorts because of the lack of lodging in those early days.

President Jefferson, affectionately referred to even today as Mr. Jefferson, was a perfectionist at growing, preparing, and serving food. He was also instrumental in introducing French cooking into the Old Dominion.

I have been to Monticello four times since beginning this book. I continue to be awed by its beauty and by the careful planning which went into every facet of its design and creation. On one visit, I stood in the dining room and imagined Thomas Jefferson standing in that very place, looking out at row after row of exquisite flowers. Today, the same flower varieties are again planted according to the precise instructions found in his journals. Resting on the branches of his "pet" trees, as Mr. Jefferson referred to them, were bright red cardinals, the state bird of Virginia. As I took in this sight, I understood why Virginians speak of Mr. Jefferson as if he lives today. His presence is still felt at Monticello.

Today in Virginia there are many inns, large and small, elegant and rustic, with innkeepers and chefs who are a proud lot. These Virginians, many transplanted from other states and countries, are dedicated to keeping alive the tradition of southern hospitality which Mr. Jefferson began.

My cook's tour was begun to gather treasured recipes from historical inns of Virginia. I traveled from one end of the state to the other, collecting firsthand the best of the best. The recipes speak for themselves, but I could not write this book without sharing my thoughts about the personality of each inn and the innkeepers and chefs who made me feel at home. Each inn was visited personally and each recipe was tested. The selected inns did not pay to be in this book. They are here because they have earned their rightful place.

My travels took me from a rustic mountainside log cabin serving fine French cuisine to the world-famous Williamsburg Inn, a five-star resort. I found that each inn had something unique to offer, from a romantic weekend hideaway to a week's stay at a rustic mountain lodge for families who want to experience a simpler life.

Now I have seen and tasted what to me is the best of Virginia. But this beautiful state has many discoveries awaiting you, so take your own cook's tour down the interstates, byways, and back roads. It will be a trip you will remember forever.

M'Layne Murphy

Monticello

Home
of
Thomas Jefferson

One of the most inspiring landmarks in Virginia is Monticello*. Thomas Jefferson chose the name — an Italian word meaning "little mountain" — for his home atop a mountain overlooking Charlottesville. From his beloved Monticello, Mr. Jefferson methodically planned his "garden," where he grew more than 250 varieties of vegetables and herbs on the southern side of the mountain. He imported seeds, vines, trees, and plants from Europe and purchased seeds from local seedsmen. The varieties of English peas harvested numbered twenty, an indication that they were Mr. Jefferson's favorite vegetable. The peach was his favorite fruit, with thirty-seven varieties recorded in his journal.

Mr. Jefferson's meticulous listings of crops and cultivation times are carefully noted in his "Farm Book." From these records, the Thomas Jefferson Memorial Foundation has recreated his "garden," where visitors are allowed to roam after a tour of the house.

A special lookout point, a brick pavilion, is located at midpoint of the stone garden wall. Here, Mr. Jefferson enjoyed the panoramic view of the countryside he loved. It was also here, perhaps, that he planned the menus for his half-Virginian, half-French dinners. Even though he was a gourmet who appreciated French food and wines — long before his tenure in Paris as minister to France — he never lost his taste for the native foods, so much a part of his Virginia.

Pronounced monti-chello.

Lemonade Iced

Make a quart of rich lemonade. (Boil 1 quart of water with 2 cups of sugar for twelve minutes. Add ⅔ cup of lemon juice, strain and cool.) Beat the whites of 6 eggs to a stiff froth. Add a pinch of salt. Stir the lemonade into this thoroughly. Freeze.

Observations on Soups

Always observe to lay your meat in the bottom of the pan with a lump of butter. Cut the herbs and vegetables very fine and lay over the meat. Cover it close and set over a slow fire. This will draw the virtue out of the herbs and roots and give the soup a different flavour from what it would have from putting the water in at first. When the gravy produced from the meat is almost dried up, fill your pan up with water. When your soup is done, take it up and when cool enough, skim off the grease quite clean. Put it on again to heat and then dish it up. When you make white soups, never put in the cream until you take it off the fire. Soup is better the second day in cool weather.

Monticello

Shown on this map of Virginia
are the locations of the historic inns
included in this "cook's tour," as well as major cities
as reference points. The addresses and phone numbers of each inn
are provided in their respective section
for your convenience. It is recommended that you
contact each inn for current room status, rates, and specific directions.
Most inns have brochures listing area activities,
points of interest, seasonal events,
and dining arrangements.

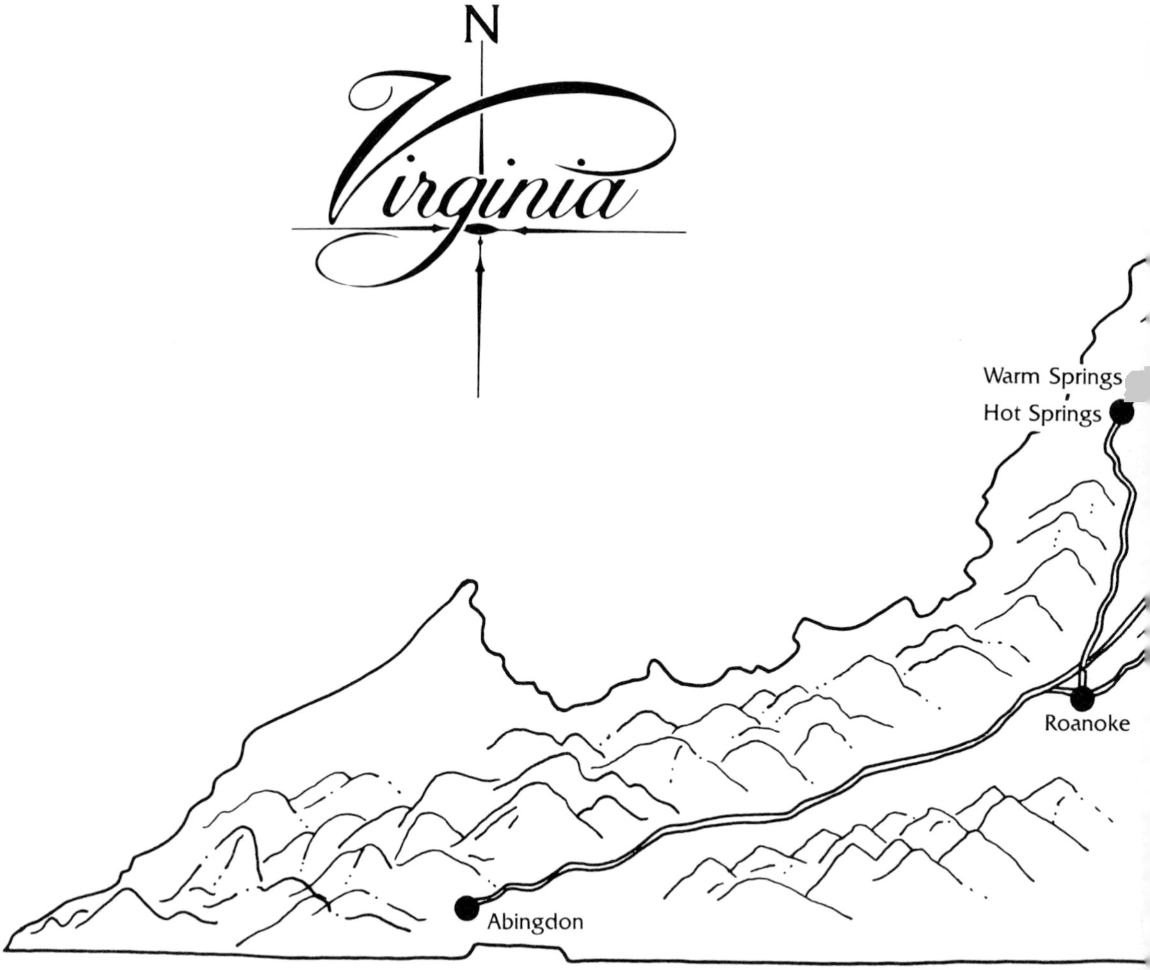

N

Virginia

Warm Springs

Hot Springs

Roanoke

Abingdon

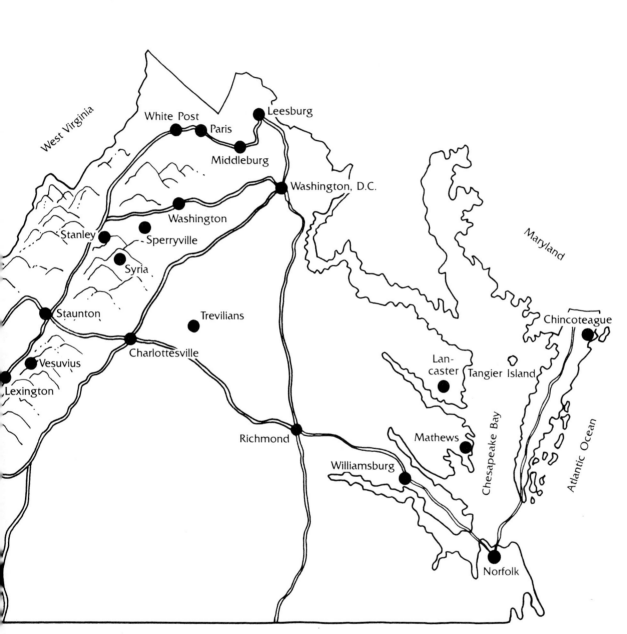

West Virginia

White Post
Paris
Middleburg
Leesburg

Washington, D.C.

Washington

Stanley
Sperryville
Syria

Maryland

Staunton

Trevilians

Charlottesville

Vesuvius
Lexington

Lan-
caster
Tangier Island

Chincoteague

Chesapeake Bay

Atlantic Ocean

Richmond

Mathews

Williamsburg

Norfolk

North Carolina

The Williamsburg Inn

Colonial Williamsburg was exactly what we expected — a major historical restoration and world-class resort. What was amazing was that the people and the history of eighteenth-century Williamsburg were never overshadowed by the enormous size of the complex and the many amenities available.

There was much to do, see, and experience — horse-drawn carriages, fife and drum corps parades, craftsmen and entertainers recreating the necessities and pleasures of American colonial life. You can walk into a real house where real people lived more than 250 years ago. You can walk down the same dirt sidewalks where George Washington, Thomas Jefferson, and Patrick Henry walked.

During a morning walk through the grounds of Colonial Williamsburg, I saw a world which spanned almost 300 years — small houses, herb gardens, arbors, fields of grain or vegetables, bowling greens, and croquet fields. Williamsburg also has swimming pools, tennis courts, a greenbelt with two golf courses, and endless tree-lined paths.

Quietly secluded by stately trees and rolling lawns is the five-star Williamsburg Inn, opened in 1937 during Williamsburg's restoration.

Rooms are spacious and decorated in the Regency style. Furniture, wall coverings, and furnishings are carefully adapted from authentic Williamsburg patterns in a resident design studio within the inn.

Every luxury is available at the inn, but you may prefer to stay in one of Williamsburg's restored residences. Choices range from a single-room dwelling to a suite with large sitting room and fireplace. My first night at Williamsburg was spent in a suite, with canopied bed designed and built for President and Mrs. Reagan for the International Economic Conference in 1983.

Style and price of accommodations vary widely, and brochures are available to help you make your decision.

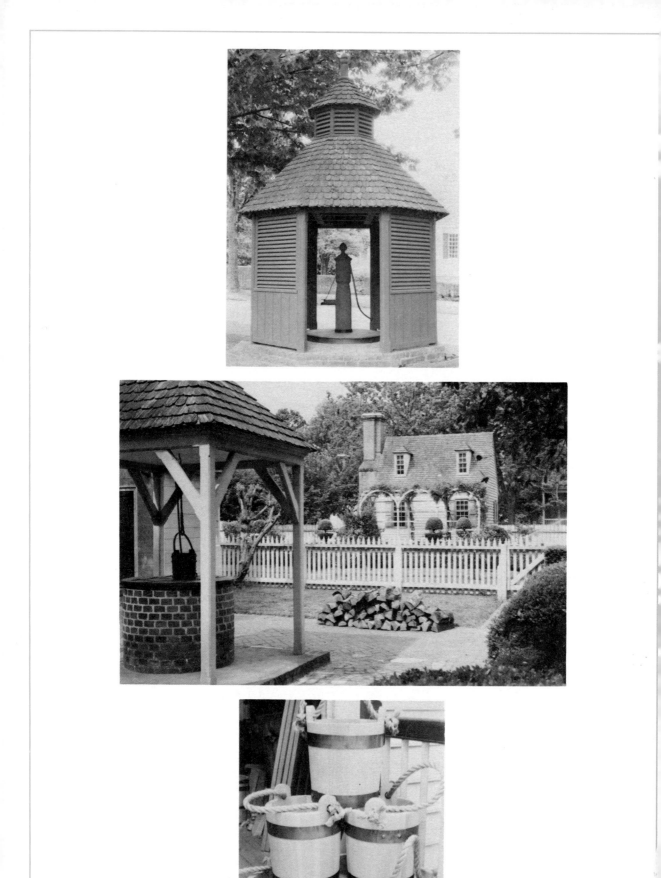

The Regency Room of the Williamsburg Inn offers gourmet dining and dancing on a grand scale.

Nothing has been overlooked, from the napkin placed quietly on your lap to the warmed cup for your after-dinner coffee to the taste and presentation of the dinner.

We were received by the executive chef, Hans Schadler, and his staff of sixty. Trained primarily in Europe and the holder of an impressive list of accomplishments, Schadler emphasized the importance of using only the freshest ingredients. His recipe for Cold Shrimp and Crabmeat Gumbo, prepared fifteen gallons at a time at the inn, includes all fresh vegetables and herbs. He also described to us the original recipe for Regency dressing, with flour base used as a preservative as it was in colonial days. Schadler's revised version has a delicately pungent flavor which made us appreciate his skills.

Williamsburg

Williamsburg was established in 1633 as a stockade to protect Jamestown, the first settlement, to the east in a marshy, indefensible location. In 1699 the capital of colonial Virginia was officially moved to the Middle Plantation, as it was known, and renamed Williamsburg in honor of King William III.

Governor Francis Nicholson, the man most responsible for the move, helped lay out the plans for the new town, "the green country town." The main thoroughfare, the Duke of Glouchester Street, was to be ninety-nine feet wide and a mile long. The College of William and Mary and the Capitol were to be on opposite ends of the street, with the Governor's Palace forming the tip of the triangle. Each house was to have a half acre for garden and arbor; the house was to be six feet from the street. This layout became the model for most American cities thereafter.

Williamsburg remained the governmental and social capital for eighty-one years until Thomas Jefferson, second governor of the Commonwealth of Virginia, moved the capital to Richmond. Williamsburg remained in relative obscurity until 1927, when John D. Rockefeller Jr. began the restoration of the historic part of the city. Today, protected and maintained by a historic foundation, Colonial Williamsburg is secure for posterity.

Williamsburg Inn

Blueberry Muffins

Yields 1½ dozen

⅓ cup vegetable shortening
1 cup sugar
2 eggs
1¾ cups all-purpose flour
2 teaspoons baking powder
½ teaspoon salt
⅔ cup milk
1½ cups fresh blueberries
1 tablespoon sugar
2 tablespoons all-purpose
flour
1 teaspoon cinnamon-and-
sugar mixture (optional)

Chef's tip: If frozen blueberries are used, toss gently in a paper towel to remove ice crystals, but do not thaw completely.

Preheat oven to 400 degrees.

Grease muffin tins 2½ inches in diameter. Cream shortening and sugar until light and fluffy. Add the eggs one at a time, beating well after each addition. Sift together the flour, baking powder, and salt. Add the dry ingredients and milk alternately, mixing just until blended. Do not overmix.

In a small bowl, toss the blueberries with sugar and flour. Add the blueberries to batter, folding just enough to mix well. Spoon into prepared muffin tins, filling each tin two-thirds full. A little cinnamon and sugar may be sprinkled on top of each muffin if desired. Bake for 20 to 25 minutes.

Willamsburg Inn

Williamsburg Inn
P.O. Box B
Williamsburg,
Virginia 23187
804-229-1000

Christiana Campbell's Tavern*

Sweet Potato Muffins

Yields 2 dozen muffins,
or 6 dozen 1½-inch muffins

½ cup butter
1¼ cups sugar
2 eggs
1¼ cups mashed canned
   sweet potatoes
1½ cups all-purpose flour
2 teaspoons baking powder
¼ teaspoon salt
1 teaspoon cinnamon
¼ teaspoon nutmeg
1 cup milk
¼ cup chopped pecans or
   walnuts
½ cup raisins, chopped

Preheat oven to 400 degrees.

Grease muffin tins. Cream the butter and sugar. Add eggs
and mix well. Blend in sweet potatoes. Sift flour with
baking powder, salt, cinnamon, and nutmeg. Add to
sweet-potato mixture, alternating with milk. Do not overmix. Fold in the nuts and raisins. Fill muffin tins two-
thirds full and bake for 25 minutes.

Chef's tip: Sweet Potato
Muffins can be frozen
and reheated.

*from *The Williamsburg Cookbook*

Williamsburg Inn

Chilled Shrimp and Crab Gumbo
Serves 12

Bouquet Garni
6 parsley stems, chopped
1 clove garlic, minced
½ teaspoon leaf thyme
½ teaspoon leaf marjoram
2 bay leaves

½ cup finely chopped celery
½ cup finely chopped onion
½ cup finely chopped green
*   pepper*
½ cup finely chopped leeks
1 pound crabmeat, cooked
1 pound baby shrimp, cooked
Pinch saffron
1 cup chopped okra
1 cup chopped tomatoes
1 teaspoon salt, or to taste
½ teaspoon white pepper
½ teaspoon gumbo filé
*   powder*
1 envelope unflavored gelatin
*   softened in ½ cup warm*
*   water*
1 cup cooked rice

Prepare a bouquet garni by tying the herbs in a cheesecloth bag. Heat 2 quarts of water to boiling and add the bouquet garni, celery, onion, green pepper, and leeks. Cover and simmer for 20 minutes. Remove the bouquet garni.

Pick over the crabmeat and remove any bits of shell or cartilage. Add the crabmeat, shrimp, and saffron to the simmering vegetables and continue to simmer slowly for 15 minutes. Add the okra, tomatoes, salt and pepper.

Remove ½ cup of the liquid from the pot, sprinkle the filé powder over it and beat thoroughly. Stir into the pot. (Be careful not to let the soup boil after the filé powder has been added or it will become stringy and unfit to serve). Remove from heat and stir in the softened gelatin. Add the cooked rice and adjust the seasoning. Refrigerate overnight if possible to bring out the flavor. Serve in chilled cups.

Chef's tip: If canned okra is used, the liquid should be added to the gumbo after the cooking process because it will enhance the flavor of the soup. If raw okra is used, blanch it in 2 cups of the stock before adding it to the gumbo.

Chef's tip: Okra will take the place of the filé powder if the latter is not available; however, gumbo tastes better when both okra and filé powder are used.

Chef's tip: Chilled Shrimp and Crab Gumbo is a delicious make-ahead recipe. Simply omit the shrimp and crab when preparing the mixture. Refrigerate until ready to serve. Flavor is best after two or three days. Add the shrimp and crab just before serving.

Williamsburg Inn

Watercress and Sorrel Vichyssoise
Serves 8

Chef's tip: This vichyssoise is even better after two days in the refrigerator. Add cream and garnishes just before serving.

Chef's tip: To make homemade chicken stock, combine all unused chicken parts, wing tips, necks, backbones, etc. with any available vegetables such as leeks, celery and onions. Add peppercorns, bay leaf, and thyme. Bring to a boil, reduce heat and simmer for 2 hours. Skim off solids which accumulate at the top. Strain mixture and reduce. Store in plastic containers in the freezer until needed.

4 tablespoons unsalted butter
1 cup diced leeks (white part only)
½ cup chopped onion
½ cup watercress, plus 2 tablespoons for garnish
½ cup sorrel, plus 2 tablespoons for garnish
3 cups peeled, thinly sliced potatoes
1 bay leaf
4 cups chicken stock
1 cup water
2 cups milk
Salt and white pepper
2 cups (1 pint) heavy cream
2 tablespoons chopped chives

Melt the butter in a heavy saucepan. In order, add leeks, onion, watercress, and sorrel, and saute over medium heat until vegetables are tender. Do not brown.

Add potatoes, bay leaf, chicken stock, and water. Bring to a boil, reduce heat and simmer, uncovered, for 20 minutes or until potatoes are soft. Discard bay leaf. Purée the soup in a food processor or blender. Return to heat and add milk. Simmer for 10 minutes. Strain if desired. Add salt and white pepper to taste. Chill thoroughly. Taste for seasoning after soup is chilled. Stir in cream just before serving. Garnish with chopped watercress, sorrel, and chives.

Williamsburg Inn

Special Regency Salad

Serves 8

2 Belgian endive
1 head Boston lettuce
1 head romaine lettuce
1 bunch watercress
1 cup Regency Dressing
16 pitted black olives, halved
16 cherry tomatoes

Cut endive crosswise into small pieces. Tear lettuce into small pieces. Remove stem ends from watercress. Toss lettuce, watercress, and endives with Regency Dressing. Garnish with halved black olives and cherry tomatoes.

Chef's tip: Substitute any other types of lettuce if they are fresh and in season.

Regency Salad Dressing

Yields 2 cups (approximately 16 servings)

¼ cup fresh tarragon soaked
  in raspberry vinegar
2 teaspoons minced onions
½ clove garlic
¾ cup vegetable oil
1 tablespoon Dijon mustard
¼ cup raspberry vinegar
2 egg yolks, lightly beaten
½ teaspoon Knorr-Swiss
  Aromat
½ teaspoon Worcestershire
  sauce
Salt and white pepper to
  taste

Chef's tip: Knorr-Swiss Aromat is a flavor enhancer available in most spice sections.

Soak tarragon in just enough raspberry vinegar to cover, and set aside. Purée onion, garlic, and ½ cup of vegetable oil in a food processor or blender. Transfer the mixture to a mixing bowl. Add mustard, vinegar, and egg yolks. Add Aromat and soaked tarragon. Add remaining vegetable oil slowly, beating constantly with an electric mixer. Beat in Worcestershire sauce, and season with salt and white pepper.

Chef's tip: Add two tablespoons of mayonnaise (preferably Hellman's) to act as a stabilizer and preservative. Dressing will keep up to 10 days if tightly wrapped and refrigerated.

Williamsburg Inn

Goat Cheese Soufflé

Serves 4 to 6

⅓ cup butter
½ cup all-purpose flour
2 cups milk
½ teaspoon salt
Dash cayenne pepper
2 cups grated sharp goat
   cheese
6 eggs, separated
1½ teaspoons dry mustard

Preheat the oven to 375 degrees.

Grease a 2-quart soufflé dish. If an especially high soufflé is desired, tie a 2-inch collar of well-buttered paper or foil around the top of the dish.

Melt butter over medium heat in a double boiler or heavy saucepan. Stir in flour and cook for 1 minute, then gradually add milk, stirring constantly until the mixture is smooth and thickened. Add salt and cayenne pepper.

Remove from heat, add cheese, and stir until cheese is melted, returning to the heat if necessary.

Beat egg yolks until they are light and fluffy and add to the cheese mixture, stirring constantly. Add mustard and allow to cool completely.

Beat egg whites until they hold stiff peaks, then gently fold the cheese mixture into the egg whites. Pour into the prepared dish and bake at 375 degrees for 15 minutes, then reduce the heat to 300 degrees and continue baking for 40 to 50 minutes. Serve immediately.

Williamsburg Inn

Veal Medallions
with Fresh Morels

Serves 4

8 veal loin medallions (3
    ounces each), lightly
    pounded
6 tablespoons clarified butter
1 teaspoon shallots
1 garlic clove, minced
½ pound fresh morels
½ cup apple brandy
½ cup heavy cream

Sauté the medallions in butter over medium heat until tender. Do not allow butter to brown. Remove to heated serving platter. To the same pan add the shallots, garlic, morels, brandy, and cream. Cook rapidly until volume is reduced by half. Cover medallions with morel cream and serve immediately.

Tip: To clarify butter, cut butter into pieces and place in a saucepan over moderate heat. As butter melts, milky solids will sink to bottom. Skim off the clear liquid and strain into a bowl or jar. (Residue may be used to enrich soups or sauces.)

Tip: If fresh morels are not available, substitute canned or dried morels. To reconstitute dried morels, add two tablespoons of apple brandy to water. This removes any harshness in the taste of the morels.

Williamsburg Inn

Chicken Monticello
Stuffed with Crabmeat and Virginia Ham

Serves 6

1 tablespoon butter
6 shallots, minced
2 apples, peeled and diced
¼ teaspoon each salt and
*   pepper, or to taste*
1 cup apple brandy

1 pound crabmeat
1 ounce Virginia ham, finely
*   diced*
6 8-ounce chicken breasts,
*   skinned and boned*
1 cup flour
4 eggs plus 2 egg yolks,
*   beaten together*

Sauce

1 cup diced celery
1 cup diced carrots
1 teaspoon thyme
2 bay leaves
2 teaspoons peppercorns
2 tablespoons tomato sauce
1 cup white wine
1 cup apple cider
½ cup apple cider vinegar
1 quart brown sauce

Garnish

1 unpeeled red apple, diced
1 unpeeled green apple,
*   diced*
1 teaspoon sugar
1 teaspoon butter

Chef's tip: A very good brown sauce can be made using Bovril Beef Concentrate, available in most grocery stores.

Preheat oven to 325 degrees.

Melt butter in a pan. Add shallots, apples, salt, and pepper. Cook over medium heat. When butter is foamy, add apple brandy. Reduce until dry. Transfer to a bowl, and add crabmeat and ham.

Pound chicken breasts flat. Season with a little salt and pepper. Spread equal portions of crabmeat-and-apple mixture on each chicken breast. Fold in half. Roll in flour, and dip in egg mixture. Place in a lightly greased pan and bake 20 to 30 minutes.

Cook vegetables for sauce in a heavy pan with thyme, bay leaves, peppercorns, and a little water until tender. Add tomato sauce. Cook for several minutes over medium heat, stirring constantly. Add wine, cider, and vinegar. Reduce by half. Add brown sauce. Simmer for 15 minutes, and strain. Serve hot over chicken, with garnish.

Williamsburg Inn

Sautéed Snapper
with Crabmeat, Mustard Grains, and Chive Sauce

Serves 4

4 snapper fillets (6 ounces each), skin removed
Juice of 1 lemon
Juice of 1 lime
½ cup flour seasoned with salt and pepper

4 tablespoons butter
½ teaspoon minced shallots
½ teaspoon minced chives
½ pound backfin crabmeat

Tip: Four 6-ounce snapper fillets will make four very generous servings.

Squeeze juice of 1 lemon and 1 lime over snapper. Dredge in seasoned flour. Sauté in 2 tablespoons of butter until tender and golden. Place on warm serving platter.

In a separate pan, melt 2 tablespoons of butter and sauté the ½ teaspoon shallots and ½ teaspoon chives. Add crabmeat and simmer a few minutes. Spoon over snapper.

Sauce

¼ cup heavy cream
2 cups white wine
Pinch cracked black pepper
½ teaspoon shallots
1 garlic clove, minced
Pinch thyme
1 bay leaf

Juice of 1 lemon
1 pound butter, at room temperature
1 teaspoon Dijon mustard
2½ teaspoons finely chopped chives

In a medium saucepan combine heavy cream, white wine, pepper, shallots, garlic, thyme, bay leaf, and juice of one lemon. Simmer and reduce until almost dry. Over medium-low heat, whip in butter (do not allow butter to break), whipping constantly until butter is melted. Strain and add mustard and chives. Serve hot over snapper.

The Tidewater Region

Originally all the land claimed by Great Britain in North America was called Virginia. Even as late as the Revolutionary War, Virginia included what is now West Virginia, Kentucky, Wisconsin, Illinois, Michigan, Ohio, Indiana, and Virginia.

In 1607, King James I sent two companies to colonize the territories. The Plymouth Company settled to the north and the London Company was sent to what became Jamestown. This first southern colony under Captain John Smith was comprised of gentlemen seeking gold. Unable or unwilling to indulge in physical labor, they were already on ships leaving for England when reinforcements bolstered their resolve to stay in the colony. Tobacco was introduced to England and quickly became fashionable, guaranteeing the financial success of the Jamestown colony. In the race to grow tobacco, the rich, coastal region began to be developed.

This area, now called the Tidewater Region, includes the eastern shore and the three hilly peninsulas — created by the Potomac, Rappahannock, York, and James rivers — which the southern aristocracy first developed. It was here that Virginians first lived as country squires on huge plantations, engaging in politics and gentlemanly sports. Here they began their lavish style of entertaining . . . an art still in existence today.

Ravenswood Inn

Ravenswood Inn
P.O. Box 250
Mathews, Virginia
23109
804-725-7272
Innkeepers: Peter and
Sally Preston

All we knew was that Ravenswood Inn was in Mathews on the East River, which flows into Chesapeake Bay. Pulling into the driveway was a delightful shock, to say the least. There basking in the sun was a two-and-a-half-story white beach house surrounded by five acres of golden buttercups. A fat white goat was tethered to the far fence, a peacock was roosting in a tree, a guinea hen raced across our path with her brood of chicks, and two dogs came bounding out to greet us. Out back we could see a hot tub perched high above the ground, and a twelve-foot sloop resting at the dock.

Sally and Peter Preston, the innkeepers, were diligently at work in the kitchen preparing for thirty-six guests that evening. They stopped and warmly welcomed us to Ravenswood. Sally is very casual and easygoing, and her enthusiasm for Ravenswood is infectious. Most recently the chef of her own cooking school in Newport News, she discovered Ravenswood while sailing the East River with Peter. When Peter retired as an Air Force intelligence officer, the couple moved in and began to restore the inn, opening in April 1985. Despite the name, Ravenswood has no ravens. The inn was named for a former owner's estate in New Jersey.

Young by Virginia standards, Ravenswood dates to the turn of the century. It was an inn and a private estate before becoming an inn again.

The restoration, according to Peter, has become an ongoing project. There are four bedrooms for guests. Two have private baths, two share a bath. On warm days you can swim or sail in the bay. The inn offers lawn games, a hammock for sunning, or bicycles to rent. On brisk days you can sit by the fire and browse through hundreds of cookbooks. In the evenings, things don't get much more boisterous than having a glass of wine in the hot tub or going for a leisurely stroll on the beach. Ravenswood is where time disappears, as well as cares.

The most important thing at Ravenswood, however, is Sally's cooking. Her style is unique, reflecting her formal training in France and Japan as well as her special fondness for Chinese food and the spicy, hearty dishes of Spain and Morocco. The herbs and most vegetables come from the Prestons' garden, and the seafood is only minutes away. Peter is very knowledgeable about wines, and Ravenswood maintains an excellent cellar. We liked the combination of quiet weekend and a continuous festive feast. I can hardly wait for the off-season to learn a few delicious tricks at one of the Prestons' weekend cooking and wine classes.

"Yum-Yum"
(Ice Cream Dessert Drink)

Serves 8

½ gallon rich vanilla ice cream, slightly softened

¾ cup Kahlúa or Tia Maria

½ cup chopped, toasted macadamia nuts

Scoop ice cream into food processor or blender. Add coffee liqueur, and blend until smooth. Pour mixture into chilled, wide-mouthed Burgundy glasses. Top with macadamia nuts. Serve immediately, with spoons.

Tip: Place ice cream in refrigerator for 10 to 15 minutes to soften. Otherwise, the ice cream near the carton will melt before the center gets soft.

Chef's tip: This dessert does not hold proper texture if made ahead and frozen in glasses. If you have the nuts chopped, it takes only a minute to prepare the actual drink.

Ravenswood Inn

Paella
(Saffron Rice with Seafood and Chicken)

Serves 8

8 hard-shelled clams	½ teaspoon freshly ground black pepper
16 mussels	
½ pound squid, cleaned and cut into rings	1 teaspoon finely chopped garlic
16 medium shrimp, unpeeled	1 medium green pepper, seeded, and cut into strips
6 cups water	
½ cup olive oil	1 large tomato, peeled, seeded, and finely chopped
1½ to 2 pounds chicken, cut into small pieces	½ cup finely chopped onion
½ pound chorizo sausage, sliced ¼-inch thick	3 cups uncooked rice
	¼ teaspoon saffron threads
¼ pound lean boneless pork, cut into small strips	½ cup fresh peas, or defrosted frozen peas
2 teaspoons salt, or to taste	8 small lobster tails

Garnish

2 lemons, cut into wedges

Scrub clams and mussels thoroughly, and set aside. Clean squid, cut into rings and set aside. With shears, make a lengthwise slit through underside of each lobster tail shell. Set aside. Shell shrimp, leaving tails intact. Reserve shells. Set shrimp aside. Cover shrimp shells with 6 cups water, and simmer for 10 to 15 minutes to make court bouillon. Strain and set aside.

Heat ¼ cup olive oil in a heavy skillet, brown chicken pieces evenly on all sides over high heat, and set aside. In the same skillet, make the sofrito: Using remaining ¼ cup olive oil, brown the chorizo and pork strips over high heat. Add 1 teaspoon salt, black pepper, garlic, green pepper, tomato, and onion. Stirring constantly, cook briskly until most of the liquid in the pan has evaporated. Set aside.

In a pan, combine the washed, uncooked rice and sofrito. Pour in the court bouillon. Sprinkle saffron evenly over the mixture. Taste liquid for seasoning, adding salt if necessary. Arrange shrimp, chicken pieces, clams, mussels, and squid on top of rice mixture.

Place pan in preheated oven or in a covered charcoal grill over medium-high heat. After about 15 minutes' cooking time, remove from oven and sprinkle peas on top. Arrange lobster tails on top. Return to oven, and cook another 15 minutes. Cook until all liquid has been absorbed by the rice, and the grains are tender. Do not stir paella after cooking begins. Total cooking time should be about 30 minutes, but it will vary. Serve with lemon wedges.

Ravenswood Inn

Gazpacho
(Cold Tomato Soup)

Serves 8 to 10

2 large tomatoes, peeled,
  seeded, and coarsely
  chopped
1 large green pepper, seeded
  and finely chopped
2 medium cucumbers,
  peeled, seeded, and
  coarsely chopped
1 clove garlic, peeled and
  minced
1 Bermuda onion, peeled
  and thinly sliced
½ cup (or more) chopped
  fresh herbs: basil, chervil,
  tarragon, chives, parsley
  (or ½ tablespoon each if
  dried)

½ cup olive oil
3 teaspoons lemon or lime
  juice
1½ teaspoons salt, or to
  taste
1 can (14 ounce) beef
  consommé
1 can (46 ounce) V-8 Juice
2 cups croutons, fried in
  olive oil

Chef's tip: In Sally Preston's recipe for Gazpacho, the vegetables are chopped rather than puréed, to provide a garden-fresh, crunchy texture. This cold soup is almost a salad.

Place all ingredients (except croutons) in large bowl, mix together, and chill in refrigerator at least four hours. Serve in chilled bowls, and top each serving with ¼ cup of croutons.

The Inn at Levelfields

Traveling up the almost endless driveway to the Inn at Levelfields, I wondered how this impressive Georgian style manor could have even been built in such an isolated area. The flat land between the Rappahannock and Potomac rivers must have been totally isolated when the original house was built over 140 years ago.

Through a chance meeting with a descendent of Thomas Sanford Dunaway, who built Levelfields for his wife, Ann Marie, I learned about the inn's fascinating history. All the building materials came from Baltimore, transported by a sailing schooner around the coast and up the icy and treacherous Rappahannock River. Then the load was transferred to oxen-drawn wagons for another long trip to the plantation.

Many other historic sights still abound in the region. Christ Church, built in 1732, is a short drive as is Stratford Hall, Robert E. Lee's birthplace, and Epping Forest, home of George Washington's mother. One of the last remaining cable drawn ferries offers a spectacular view of the beautiful Corrotoman River. Today this landmark, one of the last antebellum mansions built in the Commonwealth, is still flanked by level fields. Towering hardwood and cedar trees and a cool stream border the current fifty-four acre sight. The inn is set back from the highway at least one quarter mile and a perfect choice for a secluded get-away. The present owners-innkeepers, Warren and Doris Sadler, have carefully maintained this special, untouched feeling that attracted them to Levelfields from the start.

Accommodations include four very large rooms each with private baths and working fireplaces. They are spacious with high ceilings and large, deep windows which afford wonderful views. Lodging includes a full breakfast. Two dining rooms, one of which can be reserved for private events, are open to the public Wednesday through Saturday for dinner and for brunch on Sunday.

As we visited before the fire in the parlor, I asked the Sadlers if they missed the busy life they led in Richmond. They have no regrets. Doris, previously the owner of an antique shop and ladies' apparel shop, still enjoys exercising her design talents as well as overseeing the kitchen with the assistance of Lee Bromley, a wonderful cook from the area. If you are interested in sports, Warren Sadler, an engineer who now does private consulting, is presently the commissioner of the Mason-Dixie athletic conference for football and basketball and an avid conversationalist on his favorite subject. The Inn at Levelfields is their culmination of a dream of many years.

The Inn at Levelfields

Chicken with Irish Whiskey and Cream

Serves 6

6 chicken breast halves,
  skinless and boneless
3 tablespoons fresh lemon
  juice
½ teaspoon salt
½ teaspoon freshly ground pepper

½ teaspoon Hungarian
  Sweet Paprika
½ teaspoon dry thyme
3 tablespoons butter
¼ cup Irish Whiskey

Cream Sauce

2 tablespoons butter
¼ pound fresh mushrooms,
  finely chopped
4 medium shallots,
  finely chopped
1 medium garlic clove,
  minced
Salt and pepper to taste

½ cup dry white wine
1 cup heavy cream
2 cups chicken stock
½ teaspoons Hungarian
  Sweet Paprika
Pinch of nutmeg
Pinch of sage

Prepare the Cream Sauce first. Melt butter in a heavy saucepan over medium heat. Add mushrooms, shallots, garlic, salt and pepper. Cook until vegetables are soft, stirring occasionally. Add wine and simmer 5 minutes. Add all remaining ingredients and boil over medium heat until reduced by half, about 40 minutes. Stir occasionally.

In the meantime prepare the chicken. Pat chicken dry. Sprinkle with lemon juice. Mix salt, pepper, paprika, and thyme and rub all over chicken breasts. Heat butter in a heavy skillet over medium high heat. Add chicken and brown about 5 minutes. Turn and cook 5 minutes longer. Reduce heat to low and add whiskey. Ignite with match and shake pan until flames die. Cover pan and simmer until chicken is tender. Degrease pan juices and strain in cream sauce. Simmer sauce until thickened and reduce to consistency of heavy cream, about 15 minutes. Return chicken to skillet and heat. Serve immediately over buttered rice.

"Milkless" Oyster Stew

Serves 4

¼ cup (½ stick) butter
2 tablespoons chopped fresh
  parsley
Seasoning salt to taste

Salt and pepper to taste
1 quart fresh oysters,
  including juice

Melt butter in medium saucepan over medium heat. Add chopped parsley and seasonings, stirring with a small whisk. Immediately add oysters and liquid. Heat until oysters curl around edges. Divide oysters into four serving bowls and fill bowls with the oyster liquid. Serve immediately with crackers.

Tip: Levelfields calls this a real "oyster lover's" delight and rightly so. The oysters are left whole and are "just" cooked. They make their own liquid and their own flavor.

The Inn at Levelfields

The Inn at Levelfields
Star Route 3
P.O. Box 216
Lancaster,
Virginia 22503
804-435-6887
Innkeepers: Warren
and Doris Sadler

Sherried Crabmeat Quiche

Serves 6

*12 ounces fresh backfin
   crabmeat
2 tablespoons minced green
   onion
1 tablespoon butter
4 eggs
2 cups (1 pint) heavy cream
¾ teaspoon salt
2 tablespoons sherry
1 cup (4 oz.) Shredded
   Swiss Cheese
⅛ teaspoon cayenne pepper
1 9 inch pastry shell*

Preheat oven to 425 degrees.

Pick over crabmeat thoroughly to remove any shells and
set aside.
   Sauté onion in butter until tender. Set aside. Beat eggs
in a large bowl. Add whipping cream, salt, and sherry,
mixing well. Stir in sauteed onion, crabmeat, cheese, and
cayenne. Pour into pastry shell. Bake at 425 degrees for 15
minutes. Reduce heat to 325 degrees, and bake an additional 35 to 40 minutes. Cut and serve immediately.

Tip: When we tested,
there was enough fill-
ing left to make two
individual size quiches
as well. We also sprin-
kled a little cayenne on
the filling just before
baking for even more
color.

Bourbon Pecan Pie

Serves 6 to 8

*9 inch pie crust
4 eggs
2 cups dark corn syrup
2 tablespoons melted butter
2 tablespoons bourbon
1½ cups pecan halves*

Garnish

½ pint heavy cream,
   whipped
A few drops of bourbon
   if desired

Preheat oven to 400 degrees.

Prebake pie crust for about 8 minutes. Do not prick crust.

Beat eggs in a large bowl for 30 seconds. Slowly add syrup,
beating until well combined with eggs. Beat in melted
butter and bourbon. Stir in pecans. Pour into prebaked pie
shell and return to oven for 35 to 40 minutes, or until the
filling is firm. Serve with a tablespoon of whipped cream.
A drop or two of bourbon may be added to the whipped
cream if desired.

Tip: This is not the
usual "sweet, sweet"
pecan pie. We
thought it was excep-
tional for this reason. It
was also good with
vanilla ice cream
instead of whipped
cream.

Channel Bass Inn

Just getting to the Channel Bass Inn on Chincoteague Island is an adventure. There are no short cuts and no airports. The only flying objects are mosquitoes or an occasional missile from NASA. The most spectacular route is from Norfolk-Virginia Beach across the 17.6-mile Chesapeake Bay Bridge, (actually a series of tunnels, bridges and, four man-made islands). Then simply continue up the peninsula.

Perhaps you remember the name Chincoteague Island, home of the wild ponies, from Marguerite Henry's book, *Misty of Chincoteague*. The last Wednesday and Thursday of July, the yearly pony penning draws 10,000 or more visitors to watch the adult ponies swim the seven miles from Assateague Island.

For visitors, Assateague is a quick drive across a marshy causeway. Deer, foxes and more than ninety-two species of birds inhabit refuges. During most of the year, no cars are allowed on the grassy dunes and beaches, but cruises are available to observe the wildlife offshore. A five-mile beach on the southern end allows surf casting, swimming, and picnicking.

NASA's Goddard Space Flight Center and Wallops Launch Complex are nearby. Both are primarily research and international experimental training centers. Special tours are available.

Chincoteague itself is a fishing village which has just discovered the twentieth century. Many of the villagers, fishermen, and farmers of the famous Chesapeake Bay oysters and clams are descendants of seventeenth- and eighteenth-century English immigrants.

The Channel Bass Inn is white and pristine against its rustic background. The original 100-year-old frame house was built as an inn. In 1972 James Hanretta — owner, chef, naturalist, and musician — purchased the inn. Today, the inn has ten immaculate guest rooms, on the second and third floors, and a restaurant which has earned a Mobil four-star rating.

In the fall, Hanretta — who was trained in restaurants in Spain, France and the United States — offers three-day cooking seminars. A taste of his crab medallions may tempt you to return for lessons.

On this remote and rugged island, it is gratifying to discover an exceptional restaurant where the chef takes pride in spending hours searching for the freshest ingredients, where dinner is served by candlelight and to classical music, and where diners are attended by waiters in black tuxedos. Our only regret is not having visited years ago when, on a slow evening, Hanretta would entertain his guests with his classical guitar playing.

Channel Bass Inn

Channel Bass Inn
100 Church Street
Chincoteague,
Virginia 23336
804-336-6148
Innkeeper:
James Hanretta

Crab Medallions Espagnol

Serves 6

1 pound fresh jumbo lump
   crabmeat
Dash fresh lemon juice
2 tablespoons olive oil
1 chorizo sausage, finely
   diced
1 small onion, finely diced
½ green pepper, finely diced
3 shallots, finely diced
3 or 4 cloves of garlic,
   minced, or to taste
1 tablespoon freshly grated
   horseradish root
2 tablespoons pimento,
   minced
¼ teaspoon freshly ground
   black pepper
1 teaspoon ground cumin
1 teaspoon Worcestershire
   sauce
Generous pinch of saffron
2 eggs
½ cup fresh bread crumbs
4 tablespoons unsalted butter

Tip: We were quite surprised to find this recipe with so much seasoning to be so deliciously light and delicate. Take care not to let the medallions overcook. Overbrowning will detract from their subtlety of flavor.

Pick over crabmeat to remove all trace of shell or cartilage. Add a dash of lemon juice and refrigerate while preparing the following:

Sauté chorizo, onion, green pepper, shallots, garlic, horseradish, and pimento in olive oil until onion is tender. Remove from heat, add all spices, and cool slightly. Add eggs and mix thoroughly. Fold in the crabmeat and bread crumbs. Form into 6 patties and sauté in hot butter on each side until brown. Serve immediately.

Channel Bass Inn

Souffléed Pancakes

Yields approximately eighteen 5-inch pancakes

1½ cups all-purpose flour
⅓ cup sugar
2 teaspoons baking powder
½ teaspoon salt
4 egg yolks
2 tablespoons pure vanilla
    extract
2 tablespoons Irish Cream
    liqueur
2 tablespoons Amaretto
    liqueur
2 tablespoons Grand
    Marnier liqueur
5 egg whites
1 cup whole milk
Chopped pecans, walnuts, or
    fresh fruit (optional)
1 tablespoon butter

Sift dry ingredients together. Beat yolks. Add yolks, vanilla, and liqueurs to milk and mix thoroughly with a wire whisk. In a clean bowl, beat egg whites until stiff, but not dry. Add liquid to dry ingredients and whisk thoroughly, then gently fold in egg whites. Spoon pancakes onto buttered griddle or skillet. Sprinkle nuts or fruit on pancakes. Turn pancakes when browned, and remove when cooked in center (they will begin to get dry around the edges). For best results, do not overcook. Serve with maple syrup or preserves.

Chef's tip: A copper bowl cleaned with a mixture of salt and vinegar and then wiped dry and chilled is best for beating egg whites.

Chef's tip: Souffléed pancakes should not be cooked until bubbles dry up as with most pancakes. Carefully lift up edge to test for color. Pancakes should be approximately 1 inch high.

The Hunt Country

Horses as a way of life in Virginia date to colonial days, when the area was settled by the British gentry. Perhaps the rolling, grassy hills of Loudoun County reminded the colonists of home. The early settlers built rambling country manors in the northern Piedmont region of Virginia, and began to import fine horses. Then they brought in packs of hounds and, finally, the red foxes themselves.

Today, Loudoun County has more than 4,500 horses, a greater number than any other country in Virginia. More hunting parties are held today than in the eighteenth century. The hunt season runs from October through March. The rest of the year is devoted to horse training, horse breeding, steeplechasing, stable touring, and every other form of horse activity. This commitment to horses has preserved the lush green hills intersected by beautiful jumping-height walls built of fieldstones.

Red Fox Tavern

Stepping into the Red Fox Tavern is like stepping back 250 years to the time when this impressive stone structure served as a stagecoach stop for tired travelers between Alexandria and Winchester. Seated at a window table with sunlight streaming through the many panes, I ate a delightful lunch of crab cakes and rich apple bread pudding. The dark beamed ceilings, the rich glow of pewter and copper utensils, and the antique prints added to the atmosphere of a hunt-country tavern.

Conveniently located on the main thoroughfare in Middleburg, today's Red Fox Tavern has a sign designating it as "the oldest original inn." Its past reads like a history book. Following the Revolutionary War, Middleburg became synonymous with thoroughbred horse racing, breeding, and fox hunting. Middleburg is now known as the unofficial capital of the hunt country in Virginia.

Built in 1723 by Joseph Chinn, Mr. Chinn's Ordinary, as it was called, was a popular place for colonists. In 1887 Mr. Chinn's Ordinary became the Middleburg Inn, and in 1937 it was renamed the Red Fox Tavern. The Stray Fox Inn, a historical building adjacent to the Red Fox, is a recent addition to the original inn. The Stray Fox houses eight of the twelve guest rooms.

Turner Reuter and his family, who restored the Red Fox in 1976, have preserved the charm of the inn, carefully adding modern touches without detracting from the eighteenth-century architecture.

Each room is named for a famous person, place, or event. One such room — the J.E.B. Stuart Room — was the scene of strategy sessions between Colonel Stuart and other generals. Years later, President John F. Kennedy chose the room for a press conference.

Red Fox Tavern

The four guest rooms in the Red Fox Tavern are my favorites, but the Stray Fox runs a close second. The spacious, sunny rooms have been furnished with four-poster or canopy beds. Fresh flowers, current magazines, color televisions sets, and direct-dial phones are just a few of the extras the Red Fox provides. The *Washington Post* is delivered to your door each morning, chocolates are placed in your room at night, and terry-cloth robes are available.

The Red Fox is a pleasant drive from Washington, D.C., and only a short distance from Dulles Airport. Take a day trip and wander the streets of Middleburg, antiquing and browsing in the village's many unique shops, or plan a weekend stay. Be sure to include lunch or dinner at the Red Fox Tavern for an even more memorable impression of the beautiful region.

Red Fox Tavern

The Red Fox Tavern
2 E. Washington St.
P.O. Box 385
Middleburg,
Virginia 22117
703-687-6301
Innkeepers:
Turner Reuter
and Dana Reuter

Crab Cakes

Serves 4

5 tablespoons minced celery
5 tablespoons minced onion
2-3 teaspoons minced garlic
4 egg whites
¼ teaspoon salt, or to taste
1 tablespoon Worcestershire
  sauce
½ to 1 teaspoon Tabasco
  sauce

1 teaspoon Old Bay
  Seasoning
⅔ cup mayonnaise
1 cup fresh bread crumbs
¼ teaspoon white pepper
1 tablespoon lemon juice
1 pound lump crabmeat
Oil for frying

Mix all ingredients except crab in a bowl. Fold in crab by hand. Divide mixture into eight equal portions, and fry patties on each side until golden brown. Add more oil as necessary. Drain well on paper towels, and serve.

Chef's tip: If Old Bay Seasoning is not available, substitute ¼ teaspoon each celery salt, white pepper, ⅛ teaspoon each dry mustard, ground bay leaf, ground cardamon, mace, ginger, ground cassia bark (or cinnamon), and paprika.

Tip: Serve with lemon wedges or tartar sauce if desired.

Red Fox Tavern

Apple Bread Pudding

Serves 12

3 apples, peeled and finely chopped

2 ounces rum

½ cup brown sugar

2 croissants, cut into ½-inch squares

¼ cup currants

¼ cup mixed dried fruit

Custard

1 quart half-and-half

6 eggs

2 tablespoons pure vanilla

1 cup plus 6 tablespoons sugar

Garnish

½ pint (1 cup) whipping cream, whipped, with 2 tablespoons confectioners' sugar

Preheat oven to 350 degrees.

Peel apples and chop rather small. Place on small tray and sprinkle with rum and brown sugar. Bake approximately 45 minutes until sugar melts and apples are tender. Place croissants on another small baking sheet and bake until lightly browned, approximately 15 minutes.

Place custard ingredients in a bowl and beat with a wire whisk until well mixed. Strain through a sieve.

Place equal amounts of apple and croissant pieces in ovenproof dishes (individual or large) and mix in currants and dried fruit. (If using individual dishes, place 4 squares of toasted croissant in each dish.) Pour custard to top of dish. Put dish into a larger ovenproof container and fill with water which comes halfway up the sides of pudding dish. Bake for 45 minutes or until set. Whip cream and add confectioners' sugar. Garnish each serving with a generous tablespoon of whipped cream.

Red Fox Tavern

Brie in Phyllo

Serves 3 or 4

2 leaves phyllo pastry
4 tablespoons clarified butter
  (or more)
5 ounces Brie cheese
2 tablespoons Pistachio Nut
  Butter (see below)
6 slices challah bread
  (optional)

Preheat oven to 350 degrees.

Lay out phyllo dough and brush with clarified butter. Fold into thirds and place Brie on pastry. Pipe pistachio butter over cheese with pastry bag. Fold pastry in thirds and seal with clarified butter. Bake for 10 minutes or until golden brown. Do not overbake. Serve with challah bread, if desired.

Pistachio Nut Butter

2 ounces raw pistachios,
  shelled and peeled
½ cup (1 stick) unsalted
  butter, softened
⅛ teaspoon each salt and
  pepper, or to taste

Preheat oven to 275 degrees.

Roast peeled pistachios on a cookie sheet until golden brown, about 15 minutes. Grind in a food processor or blender until very fine. Blend with softened butter and salt and pepper to taste.

54

The Colonial Inn

Tucked among the many storefronts along historic South King Street in Leesburg is a simple, stone-framed entrance crowned with an arch of antique bricks — the entry of the Colonial Inn. Inside, the inn is exquisitely furnished with authentic eighteenth-century antiques. A wide staircase leads to ten spacious guest rooms on the second floor. Each room is individually decorated; most have two-story windows overlooking the narrow street with its unique shops and restaurants.

Fabian Saeidi, the innkeeper, has carefully blended the old and the new throughout the Colonial Inn. Although the rugs are oriental and the furnishings custom-designed to reflect the period of each room, every modern convenience is also available. The inn even has a honeymoon suite with wet bar and private Jacuzzi bath.

Saeidi, originally from Washington, D.C., came to Leesburg to open the Green Tree Restaurant with its costumed waitresses and authentic eighteenth-century food. He has added the Georgetown Café and Bakery, the King's Court Tavern, and the Colonial Inn and Restaurant.

The informal Georgetown Café and Bakery is known for its afternoon tea time. Freshly baked pastries and an assortment of teas are served from 2 to 5 p.m. daily. Just around the corner is the King's Court Tavern, a popular gathering place with a hunt-country atmosphere. The Colonial Inn Restaurant offers elegant dining in six intimate dining rooms. The restaurant is well known for the creative inspirations of its pastry chef so be sure not to miss one of his lavish temptations. Every effort has been made to re-create the grand style in which the rich and famous dined almost 200 years ago in Colonial Leesburg.

In a state known for its historic landmarks and towns, Leesburg is outstanding. Shopping, exploring the hunt country, and walking through historic Leesburg will highlight your stay at Colonial Inn.

Colonial Inn

Virginia Peanut Soup

Serves 10

½ cup butter
2 small onions, chopped
2 stalks celery, chopped
3½ tablespoons all-purpose
  flour
2 quarts homemade chicken
  stock or canned chicken
  broth
2 cups peanut butter
2 cups light cream or half-
  and-half
2 cups chopped roasted
  peanuts

Melt butter in a deep pan. Add onions and celery, and
sauté. Add flour, stirring often until blended. Add chicken
stock and stir until the liquid boils. Remove from heat and
cool for about 30 minutes. Purée chicken mixture in a
blender or food processor. Return to pan and blend in
peanut butter and cream. Garnish the soup with a generous portion of chopped peanuts, and serve.

The
Ashby Inn

Paris, Virginia, was named in honor of the Marquis de Lafayette, who visited the village after the Revolutionary War. This village of approximately sixty residents seems to have changed very little. There are only two streets — each two blocks long — on which cars are permitted. One of these is Main Street, and at one end you'll find the Ashby Inn and Tavern.

The original Ashby's Tavern across the street was frequented by young George Washington when he was a surveyor. General J.E.B. Stuart and Mosby's Raiders spent time there as well.

Ashby's is again the center of this pastoral community at the edge of the Blue Ridge Mountains. It's the only business in town and a gathering place for a sophisticated community. After dinner in the Taproom of Ashby's, you're likely to meet local residents — from "gentlemen farmers" to fine artisans to the lady who bakes and delivers wonderful bread to the inn daily.

Ashby's is only an hour's drive from Washington, D.C., through lovely hunt-country scenery. Paris is at the intersection of Routes 50 and 17, where Route 50 becomes a four-lane highway. Turn off at Route 759. Ashby's is right there nestled in the valley between the foothills, and surrounded by pastures of grazing Angus cattle and horses. The fields, which look manicured, extend to the grassy back-yard of Ashby's, where lawn games are set up. A hill separates the village from the noisy highway so we forgot it was even there.

The three-story inn has six guest rooms, all spacious and unclut-tered. Antique rugs and quilts brighten the handsome furnishings in each room. Most are from the late 1800s and were found in the nearby Shenandoah Valley. Our favorite was the Fan Room, airy and white, with skylights and a balcony overlooking the countryside where, we are told, you can often see white-tailed deer grazing with the cattle, and Canadian geese wintering on the ponds. Four rooms have private baths. The two dormer rooms share a bath. Of the several dining rooms, we preferred the casual Taproom with honor-system bar, darts, and television used only for sports.

The innkeepers are Roma and John Sherman, who renovated the inn, an 1829 residence whose architectural proportions they care-fully maintained. The fare is exceptional, with a menu part Roma, part John. Roma, a native of England, adds the robust beef-and-mushroom pie, fish stews, and Stilton cheese. John prefers country fare, including local game such as venison and duck.

The menu also varies according to the season. Sunday brunches, which bring out the entire community, may feature freshly shucked blue-point oysters and Nova Scotia salmon during the fall and winter. In the spring you may find fresh shrimp with tangy red sauce. Roma will also make a perfect omelette on the spot.

The Shermans are helpful and considerate. They will leave you alone to walk the Appalachian Trail or prepare an Ashby picnic to take to nearby Sky Meadows State Park. Horse shows, races, and stable tours are the main area attractions. You may prefer to fish, float down the Shenandoah River, go antiquing, or just walk through town.

I came away wishing we could keep the Shermans, Ashby's, and Paris our own secret hideaway. We ask only that you leave the spot just as you found it — immaculately beautiful, unhurried, and friendly.

The Ashby Inn

The Ashby Inn
and Restaurant
Route 1, Box 2A
Paris, Virginia 22130
703-592-3900
Innkeepers: John and
Roma Sherman

Fettucine
with Nova Scotia Smoked Salmon

Serves 4 as an appetizer
or 2 as an entrée

½ teaspoon butter
1 teaspoon minced shallots
⅛ teaspoon freshly cracked
  black pepper
1½ cups heavy cream
1 heaping tablespoon capers
½ pound fresh egg fettucine
¼ pound smoked salmon,
  diced
½ cup chopped scallion tops

Melt butter in a medium sauté pan and cook shallots and black pepper until shallots are translucent, about 3 minutes. Add cream and capers, and cook over high heat until sauce begins to thicken, 2 to 3 minutes.

Cook fettucine in 2 quarts of rapidly boiling water, 2 to 3 minutes. When noodles are cooked al dente (still somewhat firm in texture), drain and add them to cream sauce. Continue cooking over medium-high heat until sauce reaches a syrupy consistency. Add salmon and scallions, and toss with noodles until heated through. Pour extra sauce over the noodles and arrange the bits of salmon evenly on top.

Chef's tip: It is important to cook the fettucine in lightly salted water, since the salmon and capers lend a salty flavor to sauce.

61

The Ashby Inn

Roasted Chicken
Glazed with Dijon Mustard, Fresh Sage, and Honey

Serves 4 to 6

Marinade

½ cup Dijon mustard
1 teaspoon cracked black
  pepper
1 teaspoon mashed garlic
1 tablespoon mashed shallots
1 tablespoon minced fresh
  sage
¼ cup honey
1½ teaspoons cinnamon
½ cup Chablis
½ cup Marsala

2 3-pound chickens

Preheat oven to 400 degrees.

Mix all marinade ingredients.

With a sharp knife, remove the backbones of the chickens and split in half at the breastbones. Coat evenly with the marinade and refrigerate from 2 to 24 hours.

Arrange the chickens, skin side up, on a baking sheet. Pour remaining marinade evenly over the top. Bake for 40 minutes on the top shelf of oven. Remove from oven and let chickens cool so they can be handled (approximately 20 minutes). Remove the breastbones, ribs, and wishbones, if desired. Raise oven temperature to 425 degrees. Return semiboned chickens to top shelf, cook for 10 to 12 minutes until done, and serve.

Chef's tip: Longer marinating is preferred for the most flavor.

Chef's tip: It may be necessary to turn pan once or twice during the baking if the oven has hot spots. The honey will tend to brown too much otherwise.

Chef's tip: Chicken can be served with roasted tiny new potatoes, rice, or fettucine.

The Ashby Inn

Batterton Dark Rum Pie

Yields one 9-inch pie

Crust

¼ cup sugar
1¼ cups graham cracker
  crumbs
¼ cup butter, softened

Filling

3 egg yolks
½ cup sugar
1 cup (½ pint) whipping
  cream
1½ teaspoons unflavored
  gelatin
⅛ cup water
¼ cup Myers dark rum, or
  any dark rum

Garnish

1 ounce chocolate shavings

Preheat oven to 375 degrees.

To prepare crust, add sugar to crumbs, and mix well. Add softened butter and work into crumb mixture. Line pie plate with graham-cracker mixture, and bake for approximately 8 minutes. Remove from oven, and cool.

Beat egg yolks and sugar until light in color and fluffy, approximately 5 minutes. Whip cream until stiff, and place in refrigerator.

In a double boiler, dissolve the gelatin in water. Stir over hot water until gelatin is dissolved. Add rum to water-and-gelatin mixture, then strain into egg-and-sugar mixture, and mix well. Fold in the whipped cream, and pour into pie crust. Chill until firm. Just before serving, top filling with chocolate shavings.

Chef's tip: Roma Sherman calls this recipe mistake proof and very easy.

L'Auberge Provencale

In 1748 a young surveyor named George Washington set a white post in the ground to mark the route to the wilderness manor of Lord Thomas Fairfax. The manor was torn down in 1858, but a white post still stands, and many of the nearby residences still maintain an English country-manor feeling.

The beauty of the place captivated Celeste and Alain Borel, who were forced to land their small plane in White Post. While Alain, a fourth-generation chef from Avignon, France, attended to the repairs, Celeste explored the countryside and found the nineteenth-century stone farmhouse which soon became L'Auberge Provencale.

The farmhouse was built from fieldstones, and the woodwork was done by Hessian soldiers. Today, all the floors are original, but many of the plaster walls have been replaced. Besides the three dining rooms, the main house has two guest rooms with fireplaces. The Borels have added a four-bedroom guest house.

To Alain go our raves for two memorable meals, dinner and breakfast. Celeste, petite and vivacious, prepares the desserts and pastries, attends the extensive wine cellar, and is the hostess extraordinaire.

Celeste and Alain assured us that one of the secrets of their fabulous dishes was that so many ingredients are grown locally. They have convinced some farmers to provide them with organically grown vegetables. Perhaps most important, explained Celeste, is that herbs can be picked fresh just before a dish is prepared. The fresh flowers in profusion are also from local sources.

The Borels provided us with two menus, one for spring and one for fall and winter. What distinguishes these recipes is that they are truly gourmet dishes and yet several take only minutes to prepare, once easy advance preparations are completed. The most difficult part is finding the right ingredients. We hope you will persevere . . . the recipes from L'Auberge Provencale are more than worth it.

L'Auberge Provencale

Armenian Cucumber Soup
with Fresh Mint

Serves 4 to 6

2 medium cucumbers
Salt
1 tablespoon chopped fresh
    mint
2 tablespoons yogurt
4 cups (2 pints) heavy cream

1 tablespoon olive oil
1½ teaspoons finely chopped
    garlic
¼ teaspoon each salt and
    pepper, or to taste

Garnish

Cucumber slices
A 3-leaf mint sprig for each
    serving

Slice cucumbers lengthwise. Take out seeds. Sprinkle a little salt on both sides and set aside for 15 minutes. Rinse and drain. Slice 1½ cups cucumbers, and reserve one 2-inch-thick slice for the garnish. Steam slices 4 minutes, remove, and cool. (Do not cook slice for garnish.)

Blend cucumbers and mint in food processor or blender. In a bowl blend yogurt, cream, olive oil, garlic, salt, and pepper. Whisk in cucumber and mint mixture until well blended. Refrigerate at least 6 hours or overnight.

Slice remaining cucumber in ⅛-inch slices. Ladle chilled soup into well-chilled bowls. Place sliced cucumber gently on top of soup, garnish with fresh mint leaves, and serve.

Fiddlehead Ferns
with Wild Mushrooms

Serves 4

1 pound firm fiddlehead
    ferns (young unopened
    ferns)
⅓ pound small morels (wild
    mushrooms)
2 tablespoons butter

2 medium shallots, finely
    chopped
1 small bunch fresh chervil,
    chopped
Salt and pepper
½ cup veal stock (see Chef's
    tip page 63)

Rinse fiddleheads, and remove fuzz. Rinse and drain morels. Pat dry.

Heat butter on skillet over medium heat. Do not brown. Add morels, and sauté about 2 minutes. Add ferns, shallots, and chopped chervil, and sauté 1 minute. Salt and pepper lightly to taste. Add veal stock, cover, and simmer for 3 minutes. Serve immediately.

Chef's tip: The season for fiddlehead ferns is late March to June. They are most easily obtainable in the countryside where they grow, and in major cities.

Tip: If fresh morels are not available, substitute canned or dried morels. To reconstitute dried morels, add two tablespoons of apple brandy to water. This removes any harshness in the taste of the morels.

L'Auberge Provencale

L'Auberge Provencale
P.O. Box 119
White Post,
Virginia 22663
703-837-1375
Innkeepers: Alain and
Celeste Borel

Veal Medallions
with Pine Nuts and Basil
Serves 4

Pesto

2 bunches fresh green basil
½ cup pine nuts, toasted
½ cup grated Parmesan
    cheese
¼ cup olive oil
3 cloves garlic

Veal Medallions

4 portions veal loin (6
    ounces each), cut into 2-
    ounce medallions
Flour
2 teaspoons butter
1 lemon, quartered
1½ cups veal stock
1 cup white wine
2 medium shallots, finely
    chopped
½ cup pesto
¼ teaspoon each salt and
    pepper, or to taste

Garnish

Fresh basil leaves

Chef's tip: To prepare veal stock, brown four veal bones on a baking sheet at 375 degrees to loosen the marrow. Place bones in stockpot and cover with water. Boil for 1½ hours with bouquet garni, carrots, and celery. Strain and refrigerate. You can also use canned stock available at many gourmet grocers.

In food processor or blender, combine all pesto ingredients except olive oil, and mix until they form a paste. Slowly add olive oil until it is well incorporated. Store unused pesto in refrigerator.

Heat butter in skillet over medium heat, being careful not to brown. Dust veal with flour and sauté in two batches, squeezing the juice of one lemon wedge over each portion just before removing from heat. Keep warm.

In another skillet, combine the wine, shallots, and veal stock and reduce by two-thirds. Add pesto to reduced liquid, mix and add salt and pepper. Place medallions on plates, cover with hot sauce, and garnish with fresh basil leaves. Serve immediately.

L'Auberge Provencale

Fresh Raspberry Timbale
with Cream Cheese and Chambord Sauce
Serves 4

Sauce

8 ounces cream cheese, softened
2 tablespoons confectioners' sugar
1 cup (½ pint) whipping cream
⅓ cup Chambord or other raspberry liqueur

Timbale

1 cup milk
½ vanilla bean, split lengthwise
½ cup whipping cream
3 egg yolks
⅓ cup sugar
2 envelopes unflavored gelatin
3 tablespoons water
2 cups fresh raspberries, rinsed and patted dry

Garnish

Reserved raspberries
Mint sprigs

Whip softened cream cheese in mixing bowl at medium speed until fluffy. Add sugar, and beat 1 minute. Slowly add whipping cream and blend until smooth. Add Chambord and incorporate. Chill until ready to serve.

Place milk and vanilla bean in a saucepan. Bring to a boil, then lower heat and cover pot. Let infuse for 10 minutes. Remove bean.

Whip cream and set aside in refrigerator. Beat egg yolks and sugar at medium speed until mixture whitens and forms a ribbon. Still beating, add milk. Pour mixture into a saucepan and heat slowly, stirring constantly until liquid coats the spoon. Soften gelatin in water and immediately whisk into mixture and place in an ice bath. Whisk constantly until mixture becomes quite thick.

Carefully and quickly blend in whipped cream and gently fold in 1¾ cups raspberries. Set in buttered ramekins, small bowls, or molds. Chill at least 3 hours.

To serve, place ramekins or molds in hot towel to loosen. Turn onto chilled plates. Spoon sauce around timbales and garnish with remaining raspberries and fresh mint.

Note: Strawberries may be substituted for raspberries.

Chef's tip: If sauce appears thick, add a few teaspoons of milk, and stir.

Chef's tip: Moisten gelatin just before combining with milk mixture or it may begin to set before it is used.

Chef's tip: The consistency of the timbale mixture after whisking over ice should be much like cooked oatmeal.

L'Auberge Provencale

Escargots
with Roquefort Cream

Serves 4

2 cups (1 pint) heavy cream
1 large shallot, finely
   chopped
2 cloves garlic, finely
   chopped
3 tablespoons veal stock
4 tablespoons Roquefort
   cheese
2 tablespoons chopped fresh
   parsley
24 extra-large French
   escargots
Coarsely ground pepper to
   taste
1 cup cooked wild rice
   (prepare ahead and keep
   warm)

Chef's tip: To prepare veal stock, brown four veal bones on a baking sheet at 375 degrees to loosen the marrow. Place bones in stockpot and cover with water. Boil for 1½ hours with bouquet garni, carrots, and celery. Strain and refrigerate. You can also use canned stock available at many gourmet grocers.

Combine cream, shallot, garlic, veal stock, and Roquefort cheese in a saucepan. Heat over medium heat and reduce by one-third, whisking so the mixture does not curdle. Add chopped parsley and escargots. Add pepper.

Divide rice among four small plates and make a well in each portion. Place 6 escargots in center of each well. Pour sauce around wells and serve immediately.

Note: Do not add salt, since most Roquefort imported into the United States has salt added as a preservative.

L'Auberge Provencale

Venison Loin
Stuffed with Oyster Mushrooms and Rosemary

Serve 4

2 pounds venison loin,
cleaned and cut into four
portions (your butcher
can do this for you)
6 tablespoons (¾ stick)
butter
⅓ pound oyster mushrooms,
chopped in ¼-inch pieces
2 medium shallots, finely
chopped
1 small bunch fresh
rosemary, leaves only
½ cup water
Salt and pepper
3 tablespoons oil
2 cups veal stock
½ cup Marsala wine

Garnish

4 sprigs fresh rosemary

Preheat oven to 375 degrees.

Melt 2 tablespoons of the butter in a skillet over medium heat. Add chopped mushrooms, ½ teaspoon shallots, and rosemary. Sauté gently for 1 minute. Add water, pinch of salt, and pepper. Place lid on skillet, and cook for 4 minutes on low to medium heat. Let cool.

With a thin, sharp knife, make an incision lengthwise in each loin about 1 inch deep. Stuff opening with mushroom mixture. Fold loin over and tie with cotton string. Sprinkle with salt and pepper.

Heat oil in ovenproof skillet over high heat. Place loins in skillet and sear both sides until lightly browned. Place skillet in preheated oven and cook for 8 minutes. Remove from oven and keep warm on a hot plate.

Wipe skillet with clean, lint-free cloth such as cheesecloth. Add 2 tablespoons butter, remaining shallots, veal stock, and Marsala. Cook over medium heat until reduced by half. Remove from heat, and incorporate remaining 2 tablespoons butter.

Untie loins, slice fairly thin, and arrange in half circle on plate. Pour sauce around slices. Garnish with rosemary. Serve immediately.

Chef's tip: Domestic venison is generally tender but wild venison can be tough enough to require marinating. Rub venison with olive oil and marinate overnight in 1 cup olive oil, ¼ cup red wine vinegar, slices of carrots and celery, minced garlic, thyme, tarragon, and Herbes de Provence.

Chef's tip: Morels, shiitake, or other mushrooms can be substituted.

Chef's tip: Chef Alain Borel prepares venison stock to be used with this recipe. His veal stock (see page 67) may be substituted.

Chef's tip: Any remaining mushrooms may be reserved and added to sauce.

Chef's tip: Stuffed loins can be rubbed with olive oil and refrigerated for about two hours ahead of time.

L'Auberge Provencale

Apple Tart

Serves 8

Crust

1¾ cups all-purpose flour
½ cup sugar
¾ cup (1½ sticks) butter,
  softened

2 egg yolks
1 teaspoon vanilla
1½ tablespoons water

Filling

6 tablespoons flour
1 cup plus 3 tablespoons
  sugar
¾ cup (1½ sticks) butter,
  softened

3 eggs
1 teaspoon vanilla or almond
  extract
8 apples, cored and sliced to
  ⅛-inch thickness

Garnish

2 cups (1 pint) whipping
  cream, whipped
  or vanilla ice cream

Preheat oven to 325 degrees.

To prepare crust, mix flour, sugar, and butter on medium speed of mixer until crumbly. Add egg yolks, vanilla, and water. Knead to form a ball. Butter a 12-inch tart pan and press dough around inside of pan until it is evenly distributed.

For filling, blend flour, sugar, and butter in a mixer. Add eggs and vanilla. Blend at medium speed until mixture is pale and forms a ribbon.

Layer apple slices from rim to center, slanting them slightly. Fill crust with liquid filling. Bake for 40 minutes or until done. May be served warm or cool, with freshly whipped cream or homemade vanilla ice cream.

Chef's tip: Pears, peaches, or other fruit can be substituted for the apples. If fruit is very juicy, pat slices dry before assembling.

Chef's tip: Granny Smith or other green cooking apples are a good choice for this tart.

Inn
At
Little
Washington

Of all the celebrities you may meet at the Inn at Little Washington, one of the most fascinating is the chef, Patrick O'Connell. Along with his partner, Rheinhart Lynch, O'Connell has created a dining experience which has made him one of today's great international-celebrity chefs. The Inn at Little Washington is recognized as one of the finest inns in the world. We concur.

As we arrived for dinner, the limousines were lined up outside, but inside we could detect no preferential treatment. Every guest was treated like royalty. O'Connell recommended his six-course sampler dinner. Each course was more exquisite than the last. After a perfect evening, it was easy to understand why dinner reservations must be made at least three weeks in advance and why two months should be allowed for room availabilities.

With the completion of the inn's $2 million renovation, little is left of the original structure — once a neighborhood store, then a garage. From this humble beginning, the Inn at Little Washington has become a grand recreation of an English manor house. An intricate juxtaposition of patterns and colors made famous by the William Morris Movement is combined with faux woodwork by the foremost artist in this field. The inn has eight rooms, two major suites, and marble-and-brass bathrooms complete with extra-large towels on heated rods, terry robes, and imported soaps.

The Inn at Little Washington is a delightful contrast to its country setting. Early in the morning, mist hovers over fields covered with wild roses. Frogs croak in a nearby pond. Early-morning strollers may meet deer along the road. O'Connell and Lynch agree that Washington, Virginia, is the one place in the world where they want to live. Owning the inn is the one thing they want to do . . . luckily for the rest of us!

Inn at Little Washington

Spinach Timbale

Serves 4

2 pounds fresh spinach,
  washed, and stems
  removed
6 tablespoons butter
4 teaspoons flour
1½ cups half-and-half

1 cup heavy cream
¼ teaspoon nutmeg
1 teaspoon sugar
Salt and pepper to taste
6 eggs, beaten
Softened butter

Preheat oven to 375 degrees.

Fill a large stainless-steel pot with water and bring to a boil. Blanch spinach in slowly boiling water for 5 minutes. Cool under cold water and squeeze dry. Chop coarsely.

In a saucepan, melt butter, and stir in flour. Cook a few minutes and add spinach, half-and-half, cream, nutmeg, sugar, salt, and pepper. Let cool slightly and add eggs.

Coat eight ½-cup timbale molds or custard cups with softened butter. Fill each mold within ½ inch of top with spinach mixture.

Set timbales in baking pan and add 1 inch of hot water to the pan. Bake uncovered for 40 minutes, or until mixture has risen slightly over the top of the molds and has turned golden brown. Remove from oven and cool on a rack for about 30 minutes.

To unmold, run a knife blade around the edge of each mold. Invert a small plate over each timbale and reverse to unmold. Serve immediately.

Inn at Little Washington

Shiitake Mushrooms with Vermicelli

Serves 4

Inn at Little
Washington
Middle and
Main Streets
Washington,
Virginia 22747
703-675-3800
Innkeepers: Patrick
O'Connell and
Reinhardt Lynch

2½ cups peeled, diced
  tomatoes, fresh or canned
¼ cup tomato paste
1 tablespoon balsamic
  vinegar
⅓ cup red wine vinegar
2½ teaspoons dried thyme
½ teaspoon Herbes de
  Provence (optional)
3 tablespoons sugar
Salt to taste
Freshly ground pepper to
  taste
¼ teaspoon Tabasco sauce
1 cup plus approximately 2
  tablespoons olive oil

2 cups thinly sliced onions,
  loosely packed
2¼ teaspoons finely minced
  garlic
1¼ pounds shiitake
  mushrooms
¼ pounds vermicelli or
  capellini
2 tablespoons finely chopped
  scallions or chives
½ tablespoon sesame oil
1 teaspoon soy sauce
¼ teaspoon grated fresh
  ginger
⅛ teaspoon five-spice powder

Tip: Shiitake mush-
rooms are available
dried or canned in Ori-
ental grocery stores,
where they may be
labeled "black mush-
rooms." If using dried
mushrooms, soak them
in warm water for 30
minutes before adding
to soup.

Combine tomatoes, tomato paste, balsamic vinegar, red
wine vinegar, thyme, Herbes de Provence, sugar, salt,
pepper, and Tabasco sauce in a saucepan. Bring to a boil.

Meanwhile, heat ¼ cup olive oil in a heavy skillet and
add onions. Cook, stirring, until onions are wilted. Add to
tomato mixture and cook, stirring, about 30 minutes or
until sauce is quite thick. Add 2 teaspoons garlic and stir.
Set aside.

Cut mushrooms into thin crosswise slices. Yield should
be about 10 cups. Heat ¾ cup olive oil in a large, heavy
skillet. Add half the mushrooms, salt and pepper. Cook,
stirring often, until mushrooms are crisp, about 4 to 5
minutes.

Drain mushrooms, but reserve oil. Return oil to skillet
and add remaining mushrooms, salt, and pepper. Add
more oil if necessary. Cook until mushrooms are crisp.
Drain. Add mushrooms to tomato sauce, and stir to blend.
Let stand until cooled to room temperature.

Bring a large quantity of water to a boil and add salt.
Add vermicelli or capellini and cook about 3 minutes or to
the desired degree of doneness. Do not overcook. Drain
noodles and run under cold water until chilled. Drain
thoroughly and pour into a bowl. Add remaining olive oil,
scallions or chives, sesame oil, soy sauce, remaining ¼
teaspoon garlic, ginger, and five-spice powder. Toss to
distribute seasonings. Divide noodles among serving
dishes, top with tomato sauce, and serve.

Inn at Little Washington

Sweetbreads
with Crabmeat, Capers, and Lemon
Serves 4

4 lobes fresh sweetbreads
1 cup dry white wine
¾ cup coarsely chopped onions
¾ cup coarsely chopped celery
¾ cup coarsely chopped carrots
2 bay leaves
Salt to taste, if desired

Freshly ground pepper to taste
½ cup flour
10 tablespoons butter
2 teaspoons capers, drained
4 lemon halves
2 teaspoons Dijon mustard
½ teaspoon paprika
6 ounces lump crabmeat
1 teaspoon lemon juice

Garnish

16 thin lemon ring slices, seeded and peeled

¼ cup finely chopped fresh parsley

Cover sweetbreads with cold water and soak in refrigerator for several hours, changing water frequently. Drain.

Put sweetbreads in a large saucepan. Add wine, onions, celery, carrots, bay leaves, salt, and enough water to cover the sweetbreads. Bring to a boil and cook 5 minutes. Drain and discard cooking liquid.

Place sweetbreads on a rack in one layer. Cover with a second rack and add weights. Let stand until cool, at least 2 hours. Chill.

Pick over sweetbreads, removing membranes, filaments, or tendons. Cut each lobe into slices ¼-inch thick.

Sprinkle slices on both sides with salt and pepper. Dredge slices in flour and shake off excess.

Heat 1 tablespoon butter in a heavy skillet and add one-fourth of the sweetbread slices. Cook slices about 1 minute per side. When cooked, remove to a warm platter. Pour off excess butter. Heat another tablespoon of butter and cook another one-fourth of the sweetbread slices, continuing until all sweetbreads are cooked and on separate platters. Keep warm in an oven on low heat.

Wipe skillet. Add 2 tablespoons butter to skillet, and add capers. Cook, stirring, for about 30 seconds. Spoon equal portions of capers over each serving of sweetbreads. Sprinkle each serving with the juice of one lemon half.

Heat remaining 4 tablespoons butter, and add mustard and paprika. When mixture bubbles, add crabmeat. Sprinkle with 1 teaspoon lemon juice. Spoon equal amounts of crab mixture over each serving of sweetbreads.

To garnish, dip the rim of each lemon slice in chopped parsley. Use 4 lemon slices for each serving.

Note: Sweetbread is the thymus gland of a calf.

Chef's tip: Pressing the sweetbreads removes the lobed appearance which many people find objectionable. The delicate flavor remains.

Inn at Little Washington

Butter Pecan Ice Cream

Yields approximately ½ gallon

1¼ cups milk
3¼ cups heavy cream
½ pound (2 sticks) salted
  butter
2 cups whole pecans
12 egg yolks
1⅓ cups sugar

In a heavy pan, bring the milk and 1¼ cups heavy cream to a boil. Pour into a plastic container and cool in refrigerator.

Melt butter in a large skillet. Sauté pecans until the butter browns. Strain into a bowl. Set aside pecans. Reserve butter.

Beat egg yolks and ⅔ cup sugar with a wire whisk.

Combine 2 cups cream and ⅔ cup sugar in a heavy pan and bring to a boil. Whisk one-third of hot cream into egg yolks, then pour the mixture back into the pan with cream. Heat to just below boiling point. Stir in browned butter. Cool over ice. When cool, add milk-and-cream mixture from refrigerator. Pour into container, and freeze in ice cream freezer. Add pecans when cream begins to thicken.

Tip: This is an exceptionally rich ice cream. Small servings are recommended.

The Conyers House

Sandra Cartwright-Brown was at the stables icing the swollen leg of her horse when we arrived at the Conyers House in Sperryville. Housekeeper Debbie Racer brewed a fresh pot of coffee and lit the huge old fireplace in a friendly kitchen with walls covered with antiques and cooking implements. Scooting a stool up to the fire, I was soon attended by a tiny cock-a-poo and a cat. Another resident dog, Winchester, went to "fetch" his favorite rock.

In a few minutes Sandra came striding in, wearing jodhpurs and riding boots, her dark hair pulled neatly back, and looking much like she had just walked off the set of *National Velvet*. She gave us a quick tour of the unique rooms, each with its own name and history, filled with memorabilia, family heirlooms, travel discoveries, dried wild flowers, and Norman Cartwright-Brown's collection of stuffed birds. Much of the restoration was done by Sandra and Norman. The original structure, now the living room, dates to about 1770 and was a separate building. According to a deed from 1815, this portion was referred to as Conyer's Old Store.

Besides the five bedrooms and four bathrooms in the main house, there is also a Hill House cottage with bath, and an old Spring House with bedroom, loft, and half bath. When making reservations, be sure to ask about the various amenities and idiosyncracies of each room.

Back in the kitchen we tasted Debbie's Parsnip Cake — dark, heavy, and very good. All the Conyers House recipes are quick, zesty, no-nonsense dishes. The cornbread, beautifully pale from the addition of white cornmeal, is some of the best we've tasted. The Red Pepper Jelly is heaven.

Like so many innkeepers we have met, the Cartwright-Browns take special interest in their guests, making arrangements for them to climb "Old Rag," hike the exhilarating trails around Sperryville, or see the countryside on horseback.

You could easily make Sperryville a back-to-nature getaway retreat with the added enrichment of worldly tales and interesting conversation with the Cartwright-Browns.

The Conyers House

The Conyers House
Slate Mills Road
Sperryville,
Virginia 22740
703-987-8025
Innkeepers:
Norman and Sandra
Cartwright-Brown

Corn Bread

Serves 8

½ cup yellow cornmeal
½ cup white cornmeal
1 cup all-purpose flour
4 teaspoons baking powder
1 egg
1 cup milk
½ teaspoon salt (optional)
12 ounces corn kernels,
    drained
1 tablespoon finely chopped
    hot green peppers
1 tablespoon finely chopped
    hot red peppers
3 tablespoons butter

Preheat oven to 350 degrees.

Mix cornmeal, flour, and baking powder in a large bowl.
Add egg, milk, and salt, and mix thoroughly. Add corn
kernels and peppers. Melt butter in a cast-iron skillet over
high heat. Brush sides with butter. Pour batter into hot
skillet and bake for 35 to 40 minutes, or until golden.

Red Pepper Jelly

Makes eight 8-ounce jars

5 to 6 small red bell peppers
1 cup cider vinegar
½ cup lemon juice
5½ cups sugar, or to taste
1 teaspoon salt
1 teaspoon chili powder, or
    to taste
6 ounces liquid pectin

Chef's tip: Add more
chili powder and re-
duce sugar for a spicier,
less sweet jelly.

Wash, seed, and chop red peppers. Add 2½ cups red
pepper to vinegar and lemon juice in a large pan. Mix in
sugar, salt, and chili powder. Bring to a boil, stirring constantly. Remove from heat and add pectin. Bring to a boil
again, boil hard for 1 minute, and then turn heat to simmer. Stir, and skim off any foam. Seal in sterilized jars.

Note: Jelly will keep one year.

The Conyers House

Buckwheat Crêpes
with Sausage and Apples

Yields 4 servings of 2 crêpes each

Crêpes

¼ cup all-purpose flour
2 tablespoons buckwheat
   flour
1 egg
⅛ teaspoon salt
¼ cup milk
¼ cup plus 2 tablespoons
   water
1 tablespoon butter, melted

Filling

1 pound breakfast sausage
2 tablespoons butter
3 small apples, cored,
   peeled, and diced
½ teaspoon cinnamon
¼ cup apple cider
½ cup sour cream
1 tablespoon finely chopped
   fresh sage

Combine the two flours in a medium bowl. Mix well. Add egg and salt. Stir to make a stiff batter. Whisk in the milk, then the water a little at a time. Whisk in melted butter and set aside for 20 minutes.

Brush crêpe pan with oil. When moderately hot, pour 2 tablespoons of crêpe batter in center of pan. Immediately tilt pan in all directions to coat bottom. Cook about 1 minute or until lightly brown, then flip crêpe and cook other side. Stack crêpes on a heatproof plate, cover, and keep warm in oven.

Break sausage into small pieces and sauté in a large skillet until done. Using a slotted spoon, remove sausage and set aside. Pour off all but 2 tablespoons of grease. Add 2 tablespoons of butter and diced apples. Sprinkle with cinnamon, and sauté until slightly soft. Pour in apple cider and cook over medium heat until cider has reduced by half. Add sausage, sour cream, and sage. Stir well and heat thoroughly. Divide the mixture among eight crêpes, roll up, and serve.

Chef's tip: Serve crêpes with honey, apple-sauce, and sour cream in side dishes.

The Conyers House

Parsnip Cake
Serves 12 to 16

2¾ cups whole wheat flour
1¼ teaspoons baking soda
1 teaspoon baking powder
1 teaspoon salt
2 cups sugar, or less,
    depending on taste
½ cup (1 stick) butter
2 large eggs
1¾ cups applesauce
½ cup water
⅔ cup walnut pieces, or
    more
1 cup raisins
1 cup finely diced raw
    parsnips

Icing

¼ cup (½ stick) butter,
    melted
½ cup dark brown sugar
½ cup confectioners' sugar

Preheat oven to 350 degrees.

Butter and flour a bundt pan. Mix all dry ingredients and set aside. Cream sugar and butter, then add eggs. Add applesauce, water, walnuts, raisins, and parsnips. Add dry ingredients and mix thoroughly. Pour into prepared bundt pan and bake for approximately 40 minutes or until done. Cool, and turn out onto a cake platter.

    Combine all ingredients for icing. Ice cake when it is barely warm, allowing icing to melt down sides very slightly.

Chef's tip: This cake, which is served for afternoon tea at the Conyers House, can also be made with grated carrots.

The
Shenandoah Valley

The people of the Shenandoah Valley have one thing in common. They all profess a great love for this green, fertile valley which runs 200 miles through Virginia, banked to the west by the Allegheny Mountains and to the east by the Blue Ridge Mountains.

This area was known as "America's First Frontier." The early settlers did not come over the mountains, but through the valley from Pennsylvania — first into Winchester and then to such historic towns as Staunton and Lexington.

Highway 81 — a wonderful interstate — or U.S. 11 will take you through the valley with its limestone-dotted hills, stone farmhouses and log cabins, and picturesque towns. If you have time, take Skyline Drive, which begins at Front Royal and connects with the Blue Ridge Parkway at Waynesboro. This breathtaking drive takes you through the Shenandoah National Park. Towering trees, roaring waterfalls, and clear streams etch the countryside.

Throughout the Shenandoah Valley are many inns, some which opened in another century to serve as stopping places for settlers searching for land. Today's innkeepers are full of stories about the inns and their histories. Along the way I also discovered that the hospitality of yesteryear is alive and well in the Shenandoah Valley.

Jordan Hollow Farm Inn

When I stopped for directions a few miles from the Jordan Hollow Farm Inn, I was told by a friendly gentleman to turn right at the "stone house," as if everyone knows the landmark. I wandered down the farm roads, found the stone house, and after climbing a steep hill, saw the Jordan Hollow Farm Inn. Jordan Hollow is a "serious" horse farm in the foothills of the Blue Ridge Mountains, with views of the Shenandoah National Park and George Washington National Forest. The protected location preserves the panoramic view from commercial development.

The isolation is just one of many reasons Marley and Jetze Beers fell in love with the forty-five-acre farm. They have worked hard at restoring the beautiful colonial farmhouse with its four dining rooms — two in the 200-year-old log-cabin area, the other two in the "new" 100-year-old area. Guests may also have their meals on the veranda or under giant maple trees in the front yard.

Marley Beers raises handsome Holsteiner horses, and foals frolic with their mothers in the meadows surrounding the farmhouses.

The long porch on Rowe's Lodge, which houses lovely guest rooms, is covered with flowering vines and bordered with flowerbeds of Siberian iris.

Marley and Jetze term their food "country cosmopolitan." Marley, a former member of the Peace Corps in Africa, developed a taste for a garlic-and-cumin combination which she uses in a rib-eye steak entrée. The flavor is unique, and guests have learned to appreciate it too. Dessert could be Mother's Apple Crisp, an inn favorite and southern to the core.

While Marley is busy in the kitchen, Jetze — who is Dutch and a resident of the United States for only a few years — may challenge guests to a game of chess, or share stories about his world travels.

You will stay busy at Jordan Hollow Farm. Horseback riding year around, cross-country skiing in winter, walking, hiking, canoeing, fishing, golf, and tennis are all available nearby. Country music, dances, and picnics are featured during most holidays. However, if you are content to sit on the porch and while away the day, Jordan Hollow Farm offers prime spots for porch-sitters. No matter which way your rocker faces, the view is something to relish.

Jordan Hollow Farm Inn

Rib-eye Steak
from Travels in Africa

Serves 6

6 rib-eye steaks
3 tablespoons soy sauce
1 tablespoon minced garlic
1 teaspoon ground cumin
⅛ teaspoon freshly ground
    pepper

Mushroom Sauce

1 pound fresh mushrooms,
    sliced
½ cup (1 stick) butter

2 tablespoons white wine
⅛ teaspoon each cumin,
    granulated garlic, pepper,
    and salt

Season steaks with soy sauce, garlic, cumin, and pepper. Set aside.

Sauté mushrooms in half the butter until mushrooms give off juice, add wine, and sprinkle with seasonings. Cook until all juice has evaporated. Set aside.

Sauté seasoned steaks in remaining butter. Pour off fat as it accumulates. When done, top with mushrooms, and serve.

Note: Marley Beers became fond of cumin and garlic as seasonings while she was traveling in North Africa with the Peace Corps. This rib-eye steak recipe is the delicious result.

Mother's Apple Crisp

Serves 10 to 12

6 cups Macintosh or Granny
    Smith apples, peeled,
    cored, and sliced
⅓ cup orange juice
½ teaspoon vanilla
2 tablespoons rum or apple
    schnapps (optional)

¾ cup brown sugar
½ cup white sugar
¾ cup flour
1 teaspoon cinnamon
½ cup regular oatmeal
¼ cup chopped pecans
¾ cup (1½ sticks) butter,
    melted

Preheat oven to 325 degrees.

Butter a glass baking dish (7½- x 11½-inch) and place half the sliced apples in the dish. Mix liquids together in separate container and pour half the mixture over the apples. Mix all dry ingredients together and sprinkle half the mixture over the apples. Add the remaining apples, sprinkle with the rest of the liquids, and spread remaining dry ingredients. Drizzle melted butter on top. Bake in preheated oven for 90 minutes. Serve with freshly made whipped cream or vanilla ice cream.

Tip: Since I like spicier food than most people do, I increased the cumin slightly.

Jordan Hollow Farm Inn

Roasted Quail
with White Wine and Cream

Serves 6

Jordan Hollow
Farm Inn
Route 2, Box 375
Stanley, Virginia 22851
703-778-2285 or
703-778-2209
Innkeepers: Jetze
and Marley Beers

1 package (6 ounce) Uncle
  Ben's Wild Rice
1 apple, peeled, cored, and
  cubed
3 small carrots, cubed
12 quail (2 per person)
3 tablespoons soy sauce
1 teaspoon garlic powder
1 teaspoon dried tarragon
1/8 teaspoon finely ground
  rosemary
1 cup flour
1/4 cup grated Parmesan
  cheese
1/4 cup peanut oil

Sauce

1/4 cup white wine (Chablis
  or other dry or semidry
  wine)
1 teaspoon chicken stock base
1/8 teaspoon white pepper
2 cups heavy cream

Garnish

2 tablespoons chopped fresh
  parsley or other herbs

Preheat oven to 400 degrees.

Add apple and carrot cubes to rice, and cook according to package directions. Season quail inside and outside with soy sauce and half the garlic powder, tarragon, and rosemary. Stuff each bird with rice mixture, and reserve the remaining rice.

Mix flour, Parmesan cheese, and remaining herbs, and roll each quail lightly in mixture. Sauté in peanut oil until light brown, and place in preheated oven for 8 to 15 minutes until juice runs clear when breast is pierced. Arrange remaining rice on platter, placing quail on top, and keep warm.

Pour off all but two tablespoons of oil from sauté pan. Add wine, stirring to loosen pan drippings. Add chicken base, white pepper, and cream, and simmer until thickened. Pour over quail, garnish with parsley or other herbs, and serve.

Graves'
Mountain Lodge

Paschal Graves opened an inn near Syria, Virginia, in the early 1850s — the forerunner of today's Graves' Mountain Lodge. The original inn or "ordinary" was a stopping point for travelers to change horses before crossing the mountains. More than 130 years later and in a new location, Graves' Mountain Lodge is now a family-owned resort, a perfect haven for families who enjoy the informality and friendliness of a farm setting and country cooking. Guests can relax and take in the beauty of this special place. Take your pick of modern or old farmhouse accommodations with peach and apple orchards, farmlands, and the Blue Ridge Mountains almost at the porch step.

Jim and Rachel Graves, owners and innkeepers, have followed in the footsteps of their ancestors, especially Jim's father Elvin "Mr. Jack" Graves. The family-style meals are still served at long, narrow tables with rush-bottom chairs. The recipes have been passed down from generation to generation. The lodge offers southern family-style cooking at its best, with huge platters of food and plenty of homemade rolls and cornbread. Vegetables and fruit are grown on the Graves' farm and picked fresh the day they are served.

The Graves harvest about 100,000 bushels of apples a year. Apple-pickin' time is usually the second and third weekends of October. People come from all around at harvest time. Country music fills the air, along with the delicious smells of Brunswick stew, cornbread, apple butter, sauce, and cider. Everyone is free to roam the orchards with baskets in hand. Each year more and more families are making the apple harvest a tradition, and apple butter made the old-fashioned way in the Graves' cannery is taken home to families and friends.

For families with children who are constantly asking for something to do, Graves' Mountain Lodge is the answer. Jim and Rachel Graves provide a delightful getaway place for a family vacation.

Graves' Mountain Lodge

Corn Pudding
Serves 4 to 6

2 tablespoons butter
1 can (16 ounce) whole-
  kernel corn, drained
1 egg
1 cup milk
½ cup granulated sugar
1 teaspoon salt, or to taste

Preheat oven to 350 degrees.

Use part of the butter to butter an ovenproof casserole dish (7-inch square or equivalent). Combine corn, egg, milk, sugar, and salt. Pour into casserole and dot with remaining butter. Bake uncovered for 1 hour.

Tip: This is a fairly sweet recipe. You may wish to adjust sugar to your taste.

Chocolate Applesauce Cake
Serves 12

½ cup shortening
1½ cups sugar
2 eggs
½ teaspoon cinnamon
2 tablespoons cocoa
2 cups flour
1 teaspoon salt
1½ teaspoons baking soda
2 cups applesauce

Topping

2 tablespoons sugar
6 ounces chocolate chips
½ cup chopped nuts

Preheat oven to 350 degrees.

Cream shortening and sugar, add eggs, and blend thoroughly. Add next five ingredients and mix. Add applesauce and mix. Pour batter into a buttered 8x12-inch pan. Mix together sugar, chocolate chips, and chopped nuts and sprinkle on top of batter. Bake for 40 minutes or until done.

Graves' Mountain Lodge

Graves' Mountain
Lodge
Syria, Virginia 22743
703-923-4231
Innkeepers: Jim and
Rachel Graves

French Apple Pie

2 9-inch crusts
4 cups Winesap apples,
    cored, peeled, and sliced
    (about 6 apples)
1 cup sugar
1 cup golden raisins
1 teaspoon cinnamon
1 teaspoon nutmeg
2 tablespoons cornstarch
½ cup water

Glaze

Milk
Confectioners' sugar

Place apples, sugar, raisins, and spices in a saucepan.
Blend cornstarch with water, and stir until dissolved. Stir
into apple mixture. Cook on top of stove until thickened.
Pour into unbaked pie crust and top with remaining pastry. Bake at 350 degrees until crust is well browned.

   Brush top of pie with a glaze made of confectioners'
sugar and milk.

Tip: For extra richness,
dot the top of filling
with 2 tablespoons of
butter before covering
with pastry.

Belle Grae
Inn

In Virginia there are many country inns, some tucked out of the way in the rolling hills or perched on a mountainside, but the Belle Grae Inn in Staunton is distinctive. It enjoys its reputation as a city inn.

Staunton, a beautifully restored city, is built on seven hills, two of which were named Betsy Belle and Mary Grae by early Scottish settlers. These hills are highly visible from the Belle Grae's veranda, a perfect spot to drink morning coffee, as I did one spring morning during Garden Week. The dogwoods, azaleas, and lilacs were all in bloom during this special time of year when local gardens are opened to guests.

The Belle Grae, a seventeen-room inn, was restored to its original splendor in 1983. Michael Organ saw the building's potential and was challenged by the work it would take to complete the restoration properly. He is a proud innkeeper — rightfully so.

The mansion was built in the Federal style in 1870 by Martha Bagley, who made it her home for more than forty years. Michael confides that locals believe Mrs. Bagley's spirit remains in the house.

Many of the Belle Grae's guest rooms have comfortable canopy beds and working fireplaces. My favorite is a cozy room with high ceilings, deep windows, and an antique brass bed complemented with a pine blanket chest and armoire. The large modern baths have their original claw-foot tubs.

Weary travelers need look no farther than a nearby desk or chest for a sherry-filled crystal decanter. The many bookshelves hold a multitude of interesting titles for fireside reading. If you want company, Bell Boy, the inn's well-behaved boxer, will be more than happy to share the hearth.

Ken Hicks, the talented chef, is in charge of the dining rooms and catered affairs. Breakfasts and luncheons are served in the newly added Bistro, a bright and sunny room overlooking an expansive lawn. An adjoining terraced patio offers outdoor dining complete with umbrella tables. The Belle Grae is also a popular site for weddings and receptions, all beautifully catered by Hicks.

Dinners are served in the more formal rooms of the original house. Weather permitting, you might select a table on the veranda as I did.

The Belle Grae is on the walking tour of Staunton, which takes visitors on a stroll through history. Ambling along Frederick Street, you will pass the beautiful eight-acre campus of Stuart Hall, the oldest preparatory school for girls in the South. It was founded in 1844 as the Virginia Female Institute, with General Robert E. Lee serving as an early board member. The present name honors the wife of Civil War hero General J.E.B. Stuart. Mrs. Stuart was principal of the school from 1880 to 1899. Stuart Hall shares the educational limelight with Mary Baldwin College, a famous liberal-arts college for women founded in 1842. Be sure to visit the restored birthplace of President Woodrow Wilson at the end of Frederick Street.

The Belle Grae Inn and the city of Staunton offer travelers more than a warm welcome. They extend an invitation to come back as often as you like — an invitation I couldn't refuse.

Belle Grae Inn

The Belle Grae Inn
515 W. Frederick St.
Staunton,
Virginia 24401
703-886-5151
Innkeeper:
Michael Organ

Roast Pork Loin
with Orange Glaze
Serves 4

1 whole pork tenderloin
Olive oil
Pepper

Preheat oven to 325 degrees.

Rub tenderloin with olive oil. Sprinkle lightly with pepper. Bake pork on a rack in preheated oven, allowing 25 minutes per pound. Remove pork from oven 25 minutes before it is done, punch holes in roast, and coat with orange glaze. Return to oven and bake until done.

Orange Glaze

1 orange
¾ cup honey
½ cup brown sugar

Peel the orange and grate the rind. Juice the orange. Combine grated rind, juice, honey, and brown sugar. Mix well and coat loin. Heat remainder of glaze. Cut loin into ¼-inch slices and brush with glaze, or serve glaze on the side.

Minted New Potatoes
Serves 4

8 new potatoes
2 to 3 tablespoons olive oil
2 to 3 drops mint flavoring
1 tablespoon chopped fresh
*   mint*

Preheat oven to 350 degrees.

Oil potatoes, place on a baking sheet, and bake until done (about 30 minutes). Remove from oven and cool. Cut potatoes in half.

In a large cast-iron skillet, heat enough olive oil to cover the bottom. Using medium heat, place potatoes in skillet when oil is hot. (Do not allow oil to smoke.) Toss potatoes in skillet until they are lightly browned. Turn off heat and cool for 5 minutes. Add mint flavoring and fresh mint. Toss and reheat before serving.

Chef's tip: These potatoes are excellent with pork, seafood, or lamb.

Belle Grae Inn

Poppy Seed Bread

Yields 3 loaves

3 cups all-purpose four
1½ teaspoon salt
2¼ cups sugar
1½ tablespoons poppy seeds
1½ teaspoons baking
   powder
3 eggs

1½ cup milk
1⅛ cup oil
1½ teaspoon vanilla
1½ teaspoon almond
   flavoring
1½ teaspoon butter
   flavoring

Preheat oven to 350 degrees.

Mix all ingredients 1 or 2 minutes with electric mixer on medium speed. Pour into three lightly oiled loaf pans (approximately 8½ × 4½ × 2½) or one bundt pan. Bake 1 hour or until the toothpick comes out clean. Top will crack. Allow to cool approximately 5 minutes before glazing.

Glaze

¼ cup orange juice
¾ cup sugar
½ teaspoon vanilla
½ teaspoon almond
   flavoring
½ teaspoon butter flavoring

Heat all ingredients together until sugar dissolves. Let cake cool about 5 minutes. Brush or pour glaze over the warm cakes.

Tip: Very good cake for breakfast or tea.

Chef's tip: Be sure to use butter flavoring. Adds more moisture and flavor than butter.

Chef's tip: Cake should not be overcooked. Toothpick does not have to come out entirely clean.

Chef's tip: Punch small holes in cake so glaze can seep down into cake for added flavor.

Chef's tip: This cake is even better after being frozen.

The Boar's Head Inn

The night of my stay at the Boar's Head Inn, I watched a late-spring storm over the Blue Ridge Mountains. The view from my balcony, overlooking a crystal-clear lake, was breathtaking. The ducks and solitary swan seemed oblivious to the approaching storm.

By the dinner hour the storm had intensified, and in the midst of the second course, a power failure occurred. Hundreds of candles were placed in the dining rooms, stairways, and hallways. Chef Melvin Frye of the Boar's Head Inn and the entire hotel staff deserved kudos for their flawless service during a modern-day crisis.

The Boar's Head Inn resembles a country estate overlooking its own private lake — only minutes from a busy bypass leading into Charlottesville. At this large inn of 175 rooms, guests are welcomed in a small lobby, like the foyer of an English inn.

The Old Mill Dining Room and a comfortable social room, "The Ordinary," contain pine beams, flooring, and paneling from a gristmill bought by John Rogan, owner of the Boar's Head. The gristmill was built in 1834 on the Hardware River. During the Civil War — when Generals Grant and Custer marched through Charlottesville destroying all manufacturing facilities — the gristmill was spared. After the Civil War it was operated by a retired Confederate general for more than sixty years. When Rogan purchased the mill it was removed, piece by piece, and rebuilt on the present site of the Boar's Head Inn.

The Boar's Head Inn staff has a special talent for planning events tied to each season. There's ballooning over the flowering dogwood trees in spring or over the brilliant-colored fall foliage. Summer has warm days for sports, but cool mountain breezes in the evenings. The Albemarle Harvest Wine Festival is in the fall; the blessing of hounds is held before Thanksgiving; and the Merrie Olde England Festival is just before Christmas.

Chef Frye's culinary expertise is especially evident during the holidays. The inn is transformed with wonderful smells from the kitchens, the scent of freshly cut pine everywhere, roaring fires, and "mumming" activities which include caroling, plays, instrumental music, dancing, and wassailing. The "Feast Before Forks" menu includes authentic medieval recipes — Cornish Brydys, Mooton-y-Chopt, and Pudding of Plumme.

Frye, who began his career at Boar's Head Inn more than seventeen years ago, places special emphasis on ingredients raised locally. In his delicious Rabbit and Shiitake Soup, he uses shiitake mushrooms grown in neighboring Buckingham County. The rabbits are fresh, not frozen, and are raised near Charlottesville. Frye has perfected the cooking of famous Virginia country hams — served with red-eye gravy for breakfast, combined with raisin sauce for an entrée, or used in a Ham Dijon Pâté for a balloon picnic.

Country Ham and Dijon Pâté

Serves 10 to 20

2 pounds country ham,
  cooked and ground
5 stalks celery, finely
  chopped
1 medium onion, finely
  chopped
1 tablespoon chopped parsley
½ cup fresh bread crumbs
1 tablespoon white pepper
⅓ cup Dijon mustard
3 eggs
Butter or thinly sliced
  fatback

Preheat oven to 350 degrees.

Mix the ham and chopped vegetables. Add the remaining ingredients and set aside. Butter the inside of a 1-quart ovenproof dish or mold, or line with fatback sliced very thin. Fill the dish with the ham mixture and set it inside a larger container filled with water which comes halfway up the sides of the pâté dish. Cover both containers with foil. Bake for 45 minutes. Allow to cool slightly before unmolding.

The Boar's Head Inn Ham

The Boar's Head Inn has been buying Virginia country hams from the number-one Ham Man — Jim Kite — for many years. We decided to find out just what made Virginia country hams so special, so off we headed for Wolftown and Jim Kite.

In a short time, we learned more about Virginia country hams than we ever thought was possible. The hams are first rolled in what Jim calls "cure" — salt, sugar, and nitrate. Then the hams are refrigerated at a temperature of not more than 40 degrees for one week. After a week, the hams are individually handled and "overhauled" for a second roll in the "cure." Back they go in the walk-in refrigerator for a month. Afterwards, the hams are placed in nets to hang.

There are three degrees of curing, each giving its own distinctive taste, much like cheese which is mild, mellow, or sharp. Hams which hang for three months are mild and best for frying. The medium-flavor hams hang for five to eight months. The sharp hams, which are very salty, hang for eight months to a year. For guests who want to send a taste of Virginia back home, the Boar's Head Inn Store will ship the hams anywhere. The people at Kite's Hams offered this tip for maintaining a ham's flavor at home: always cut the ham from the hock, not the center. Otherwise the ham will dry out.

To Boil a Ham

Ham should be washed and soaked all night in cold water. The next morning, scrape and wash well, put on to boil in water to cover it more than well. Boil for five, six, or seven hours. It is not done until the bone in the underpart comes off with ease. But it is best not to boil it until the meat is in strings.

Hams improve in flavor until they are two years old. After that they are neither better nor worse.

Monticello

Oakencroft Vineyard and Winery, owned by Mrs. John B. Rogan, is just a short, pleasant drive from the Boar's Head Inn. Located in the Monticello Viticultural Area, Oakencroft is one of the ten licensed wineries dedicated to bringing to reality Thomas Jefferson's dream of producing quality wines in Virginia.

Mr. Jefferson, a connoisseur of wines, regarded them as "a necessity of life" and described in his journals more than twenty varieties of grapes he was growing in his Monticello vineyard in 1807.

A visit to the winery and vineyard — with its red barn nestled among green, rolling hills — can easily be included in any tour of Mr. Jefferson's country. Tours and tastings are by appointment only.

The Boar's Head Inn
Route 250 West
P.O. Box 5185
Charlottesville,
Virginia 22905
804-296-2181
Innkeeper: Jerald
Godin

The Boar's Head Inn

Rabbit and Shiitake Soup

Serves 6 to 8

1 small rabbit
3 tablespoons butter
⅓ cup finely chopped celery
⅓ cup finely chopped onions
⅓ cup finely chopped carrots
1 tablespoon poultry
   seasoning
1 tablespoon thyme
Salt and freshly ground
   pepper to taste
½ cup thinly sliced shiitake
   mushrooms
1 tablespoon chopped parsley

Bone the rabbit and dice meat very finely. Put bones and scraps in a saucepan and half cover with water. Simmer for about an hour to make stock. Strain and reserve liquid.

Melt 2 tablespoons butter in a heavy pan and sauté celery, onions, and carrots. Add stock to vegetables. Add poultry seasoning, thyme, salt and pepper, and simmer 10 to 15 minutes.

Melt remaining tablespoon of butter in a skillet and sauté mushrooms. Just before serving, float mushrooms on top of soup and garnish with parsley.

Tip: Shiitake mushrooms are available dried or canned in Oriental grocery stores, where they may be labeled "black mushrooms." If using dried mushrooms, soak them in warm water for 30 minutes before adding to soup.

The Boar's Head Inn

Stuffed Breast of Duck
with Gouda Cheese Sauce
Serves 4

2 whole duck breasts, boned
4 slices prosciutto ham
4 ounces Gouda cheese,
  grated
8 ounces roasted hazelnuts
4 tablespoons butter, melted
Salt and pepper
2 cups Gouda Cheese Sauce

Preheat oven to 350 degrees.

Pound the duck breasts very thin. Lay a slice of prosciutto on each breast. Mix cheese and hazelnuts until well blended. Divide the mixture into four equal parts then stuff each duck breast. Roll up. Season with salt and pepper. Dust lightly with flour and place in baking pan. Butter the tip of each breast. Bake for about 30 minutes.
Prepare Gouda Cheese Sauce.
When duck breasts are cooked, slice each in half and top with cheese sauce for serving.

Tip: Duck breasts usually come whole. You will need to split in half, remove bone and skin before pounding thin.

Tip: This recipe is also delicious with chicken substituted for duck.

Gouda Cheese Sauce

2 tablespoons unsalted butter
2 tablespoons flour
2 cups milk
Salt and pepper to taste
8 ounces gouda cheese,
  grated

Melt butter in thick-bottomed pan and add flour, stirring to form roux. Cook roux for 2 minutes over low heat. Heat milk to a light boil, then gradually stir it into roux, whisking briskly. Simmer for 5 minutes, and strain. Add salt and pepper to taste. Simmer for a few minutes over low heat and add gouda. Stir until cheese is melted and sauce is smooth. Pour over duck and serve.

The Boar's Head Inn

Cottage Dill Rolls
Yields 12 large rolls

Tip: The cottage cheese gives these dill rolls a wonderful flavor, similar to sourdough bread. Since they require no rising, we timed them to come out of the oven piping hot at the same time as our entrée.

1 pound small-curd cottage
    cheese
2½ tablespoons sugar
1 tablespoon finely chopped
    onion
2 tablespoons butter, softened
1 teaspoon salt
1 teaspoon finely chopped
    fresh dill
½ teaspoon baking soda
1 egg
1 tablespoon horseradish
1½ ounce cake yeast (or ¾
    ounce dry)
½ cup water
3½ cups bread flour
2 tablespoons butter, melted
Additional melted butter for
    brushing tops of baked
    rolls

Preheat oven to 350 degrees.

Mix cottage cheese, sugar, onion, butter, salt, dill, soda, egg, and horseradish together in mixer with paddle attachment or at slow speed with regular beater. Add remaining ingredients and mix with a dough hook until well mixed, or knead by hand for 10 minutes. Add any additional flour needed to prevent sticking.

Shape into rolls and bake for 30 minutes or until golden brown. Rolls should sound hollow when tapped. Brush with melted butter when done. Serve immediately.

Tip: Using small-curd cottage cheese instead of large curd produces a finer-textured roll.

110

The Boar's Head Inn

Fresh Raspberry Ice Cream
Serves 8 to 10

4 cups (2 pints) fresh
  raspberries
3 eggs
1⅓ cups sugar
1¼ cups light corn syrup
1½ cups heavy cream
1 cup half-and-half
1 tablespoon lemon juice
3 tablespoons Chambord (or
  other raspberry liqueur)

Wash and purée raspberries. Strain the seeds out and discard. Beat eggs and sugar well. Add remaining ingredients and raspberry purée. Freeze in an ice-cream maker as directed.

Raspberry Sauce

2 cups (1 pint) fresh
  raspberries
⅔ cup granulated sugar
2 to 4 tablespoons Chambord
  and cognac

Clean and purée the raspberries. Strain the seeds out and discard. Add the sugar and blend until sugar is completely dissolved. Add the raspberry liqueur and cognac to taste.

Chef's tip: If sauce is not thick enough, heat slightly and thicken with a mixture of corn-starch and water.

Silver Thatch Inn

Silver Thatch Inn, a charming colonial structure dating from 1780, is only minutes from the heart of Charlottesville and a "heartbeat" away from the airport. For travelers who want a small, conveniently located inn with an interesting history and personable innkeepers, the Silver Thatch is a perfect choice.

A wide, antique-brick walkway leads to the entrance of this sparkling-white clapboard house with deep-green shutters. The oldest section of the house was built by Hessian soldiers who were taken prisoner during the Revolutionary War at the battle of Saratoga, New York. They were marched south to Charlottesville and instructed to build their own barracks. The two-story log cabin, built on the site of a former Indian settlement, is in the section of the house which contains a dining room named the Hessian Room. The timber in this quaint, cozy room is original from 1780. The center part of the house, built in 1812, served as a boys' school for many years. During the latter nineteenth century, the property was used for a variety of purposes. At one time it was a tobacco plantation, and after the Civil War it was a melon farm. The final wing of the house was added in 1937 by a former dean of the University of Virginia, who made it his home until 1969.

The present owners are Tim and Shelley Dwight, an attractive young couple who came to Virginia from New Jersey. Their dream of an inn with a fine restaurant took them on a search which lasted many months, over many miles from the top of Maine to the tip of Florida. They finally chose the property now known as Silver Thatch. Tim's background in hotel management and Shelley's as a French chef are a perfect combination for the couple to become successful innkeepers.

Upstairs, above the three dining rooms and comfortable bar, are five spacious guest rooms with high ceilings, stenciling, country quilts, and antique furniture. You can sense the importance the Dwights have placed on maintaining the old and blending the new by the recent addition of a guest cottage which is architecturally compatible.

Shelley Dwight, an innovative chef, changes the menu monthly, selecting dishes appropriate to the season. In addition to the more traditional dishes on the menu, she tempts diners with unique offerings such as Thai-spiced duckling and black-walnut pasta. While enjoying dinner at the Silver Thatch, I visited with the owners of the Boar's Head Inn and the owner of the Oakencroft Vineyards, who were seated at a nearby table. What better recommendation is there than to have other innkeepers and owners dine at your restaurant? Tim Dwight's friendly manner and Shelley Dwight's talents as a chef keep travelers and residents of Charlottesville coming back for more.

Silver Thatch Inn

Mushrooms Albemarle

Serves 4 to 6

*24 small mushrooms, 1-inch
  diameter*
*1 pound pork sausage,
  crumbled*
1 tablespoon olive oil
½ cup chopped scallion tops
½ teaspoon chopped shallots
½ teaspoon chopped garlic
¼ teaspoon salt
¼ teaspoon pepper
*1 teaspoon finely chopped
  fresh basil, or ½ teaspoon
  dried*
*½ cup grated Parmesan
  cheese*
*¾ pound grated mozzarella
  or fontina cheese*

Preheat oven to 350 degrees.

Poach mushroom caps in water or stock until lightly cooked. Drain, cool, and set aside.

In a sauté pan, cook pork sausage. Drain well and crumble into small pieces. Set aside. Add oil to pan, and sauté scallions, shallots, and garlic. Season with salt, pepper, and basil. Add sausage and Parmesan to pan, mix well, and remove from heat.

Place mushroom caps in an ovenproof casserole. Top with sausage mixture and grated mozzarella or fontina cheese. Bake for 15 minutes or until cheese is melted and golden. Serve immediately.

Mint Sauce for Lamb

Serves 4 to 6

½ cup sugar
¼ cup white wine vinegar
¼ cup water
1 jar (10 ounce) mint jelly
*1 cup finely chopped fresh
  mint leaves*

Mix sugar, vinegar, and water in a saucepan and heat at medium temperature. When sugar dissolves, add jelly and simmer until jelly is completely melted. Add mint leaves and serve immediately.

Chef's tip: The Silver Thatch Inn serves this easy, fresh mint jelly with grilled lamb chops, but it goes well with any cut of lamb.

Chef's tip: When served warm, the sauce is syrupy in consistency. If allowed to cool, it will thicken into a jelly.

Silver Thatch Inn

The Silver Thatch Inn
3001 Hollymead Road
Charlottesville,
Virginia 22901
804-978-4686
Innkeepers: Tim and
Shelley Dwight

Fettuccine with Duck

Serves 6

1 pound fettuccine (fresh or
  frozen), cooked and
  drained
4 tablespoons butter
1 5-pound fresh duck,
  skinned, boned and diced
1 tablespoon marjoram
1 tablespoon thyme
1 tablespoon basil
1 clove garlic, finely chopped
2 shallots, finely chopped
1 red pepper, sliced in
  julienne strips (reserve 3
  slices per serving)

1 green pepper, sliced in
  julienne strips (reserve 3
  slices per serving)
1 pound mushrooms, sliced
  in julienne strips
1 tablespoon tomato paste
2 cups (1 pint) heavy cream
½ cup Parmesan cheese,
  grated
¼ teaspoon each salt and
  pepper, or to taste
2 tablespoons flour

Garnish

Blanched red and green
  peppers

Chopped parsley

Tip: This recipe can also
be prepared with chic-
ken or pheasant.

Cook fettuccine according to directions, rinse, and set
aside. Melt 1 tablespoon of butter in skillet and, sauté duck
with marjoram, thyme, and basil for 5 minutes or until
medium rare.

In a separate pan, melt 1 tablespoon butter. Add garlic,
shallots, peppers, and mushrooms, and sauté until
tender. Add tomato paste, cream, Parmesan, salt, and
pepper.

In a small skillet melt the remaining 2 tablespoons of
butter over low heat. Stir in flour to make a paste. Slowly
add water, stirring constantly to form a roux. Add roux to
the cream sauce to thicken it. Add cooked pasta to cream
sauce and heat while heating the duck.

To serve, put pasta and cream sauce in a large soup
plate, place duck around the rim, and garnish with the
blanched julienne peppers and chopped parsley.

Tip: Quickly blanch the
peppers by placing
them in boiling water
for 1 minute to soften
their crispness slightly
and brighten their col-
ors.

Inn at Prospect Hill

The moment I turned into the box-wood-edged lane leading to the Inn at Prospect Hill, I knew I had made an exciting discovery. Tasteful signs on the brick posts at the entrance give guests the feeling they have arrived at a very secluded estate for a memorable stay.

Built in 1732, the main plantation house is shaded by trees. Fortunately, the outbuildings were retained over the years. Bill and Mireille Sheehan, owners and innkeepers since 1977, told me these cottages are now favorite accommodations with those who like extra privacy.

The oldest original house is a log cabin of original hewed logs dating from about 1699. As the families of the plantation owners grew in size, the older boys, who stayed home to work the land, were given the "boys' cabin." Today, almost 300 years later, the name remains.

The overseer's cottage is a three-room suite with its own front porch, complete with a swing and rocking chair. The bedroom has two walls of windows which overlook an expansive lawn and swimming pool.

Prospect Hill enables guests to leave behind the busy, modern world and discover what Bill Sheehan calls "a special serenity." Originally from New York City, Bill and his French wife, Mireille, honeymooned in Virginia. They never forgot the serenity of the place, and years later — after five years of searching for the perfect inn — they purchased Prospect Hill. Their goal was to have an inn which was elegant but not pretentious. This has certainly been accomplished.

Inn
at
Prospect Hill

From the warm welcome to the "Good-bye until next time," the Sheehans' version of southern hospitality prevails. Their special touches — from wine, cheese, and fruit in your room to steaming coffee served in a heated cup — are part of what makes them such gracious hosts. Prospect Hill is an inn that serves guests first, with additional tables for local people or travelers. Reservations are a must and holidays are booked months in advance.

Prospect Hill is one of 13 plantations belonging to the Green Springs National Historic District. The famous eighteenth-century spa is a mile away. The Sheehans are only the fourth family to own Prospect Hill since 1699. After the Civil War — known in the county as "the War in the Defense of Virginia" — the Overton family took in guests — first cousins and other family members, and, eventually, travelers. They never advertised or used a set tariff. Envelopes were placed in the rooms and guests left what they could afford during this difficult time of Reconstruction of the South.

Bill Sheehan, a history buff of the Old Dominion, enjoys sharing his knowledge with guests. Cooking was his hobby before he became an innkeeper. Many of the inn's special recipes are ones that Mireille brought from France.

While Bill is busy in the kitchen preparing dinner, guests may visit on the veranda and enjoy the view — or in winter, they can sit by a roaring fire with classical music setting the mood for the evening.

At eight o'clock Bill rings the dinner bell and announces the menu. He is quick to tell quests that there is only one entrée each evening. If you were cooking for friends you would not give them a choice of entrées, so Bill does not. If you have special diet requirements, however, he will make exceptions. Whatever the chef prepares for dinner will be a taste treat — a meal to be remembered.

Inn at Prospect Hill

Salad Vinaigrette
(Prospect Hill House Salad)
Serves 12 to 20

5 heads Boston or Bibb
lettuce, preferably
hydroponic (allow 2 or 3
servings per head)
¼ cup olive oil
¼ cup vegetable oil
¼ cup red wine vinegar
3 cloves garlic, minced
¼ teaspoon salt
½ teaspoon dried basil
1 egg yolk
Cherry tomatoes
Tiny black olives (from Nice,
France)
Hard-boiled egg wedges

Have all ingredients at room temperature. Wash and dry lettuce leaves. Whisk together oils and vinegar. In mortar and pestle, crush garlic with salt and whisk in oil. Just prior to serving, whisk in basil and egg yolk. Pour dressing over salad, toss with your hands, and garnish with tomatoes, olives, and egg wedges.

Chef's tip: All ingredient portions can be adjusted to suit your taste.

Inn at Prospect Hill

Inn at Prospect Hill
Route 1, Box 55
Trevilians,
Virginia 23170
703-967-0844
Innkeepers: Bill and
Mireille Sheehan

Tournedos Prospect Hill
with Onions, Mushrooms and Prosciutto Ham

Serves 4

4 filet mignon steaks, 1½ to
*   2 inches thick, trimmed*
8 large mushrooms
2 ounces prosciutto ham (1
*   or 2 slices)*
2 tablespoons butter
½ small onion, chopped
2 tablespoons bread crumbs
1 tablespoon port wine
1 cup brown gravy

Garnish

Green onions
Cherry tomatoes

Preheat oven to 400 degrees.

Remove stems from mushrooms. Chop stems finely and reserve caps. Chop prosciutto as finely as possible. Melt butter and sauté onion, chopped mushroom stems, and ham for 5 minutes or until onion is soft. Add bread crumbs and mix well. Brush mushroom caps with melted butter inside and out and fill with cooked mixture. Bake 15 minutes.

In a large skillet sear steaks over very high heat until medium rare (120-degrees on a meat thermometer). Remove steaks to serving platter and keep warm in 120 degree oven. Deglaze the skillet by scraping the bottom with spoon as you pour in the port wine. Add gravy and heat. Place cooked mushroom caps over steaks and pour sauce over all. Garnish with green onions and cherry tomatoes.

Chef's tip: Cold steaks take a long time to cook. Leave them on a covered platter to come to room temperature. Use a good meat thermometer to check for doneness.

Chef's tip: To make a quick and very acceptable brown gravy, heat a can of Crosse & Blackwell oxtail soup with 1 tablespoon of port or Madeira wine.

Chef's tip: Filets are best seared in a heavy cast-iron skillet sprinkled with salt and pepper. Searing at high heat locks in the natural juices.

Chocolate Chiffon Cake
Filled with Whipped Cream
Serves 10 to 12

2 cups cake flour
1¾ cups sugar
½ cup cocoa powder
3 teaspoons baking powder
½ cup (1 stick) butter,
  melted
7 eggs, separated
¾ cup water
½ teaspoon cream of tartar
1 teaspoon vanilla extract
1 cup (½ pint) whipping
  cream
1 envelope unflavored gelatin
  (optional)
Cognac, Grand Marnier, or
  other liqueur (optional)
Confectioners' sugar
Shaved chocolate or
  mandarin orange sections
  (optional)

Preheat oven to 325 degrees.

Mix dry ingredients in large bowl and add melted butter, egg yolks, and water, and blend. (Do not overbeat.)

Beat egg whites with cream of tartar until stiff, but not dry. Fold into cake mixture. Pour into a 10- or 12-inch springform pan and bake approximately 1 hour (or until toothpick inserted in center is clean). Cool on cake rack.

Just prior to serving, split cake and remove top. Whip cream with confectioners' sugar and gelatin, if using it. Sprinkle cake with liqueur if you wish and spread with whipped cream. Replace top, slice, and sprinkle with confectioners' sugar. Garnish with shaved chocolate or mandarin orange sections if desired.

Chef's tip: Cake should not be made any earlier than the morning before the evening it will be served. The cake should be split and spread with whipped cream not more than 30 minutes prior to serving.

Chef's tip: Adding the unflavored gelatin to the whipping cream maintains the form of the filling. Let gelatin soak in cream for 10 minutes before whipping.

Tip: Put mixing bowl, beaters, and cream in freezer for 30 minutes before beating (especially in summer or if kitchen is warmer than 70 degrees F).

Chef's tip: Place cake upside down on serving platter before releasing springform pan. Leave bottom of pan on top of cake. Slice cake in half. Remove pan bottom and slide under top layer. This method provides a moister cake than baking the cake in two separate pans.

Chef's tip: Once the cake is spread with whipping cream and the top replaced, slice the cake into the desired number of portions and sprinkle the entire cake top with confectioners' sugar for a more attractive cake.

Inn at Prospect Hill

Apricot Cream Tart

Serves 12 to 14

2 9-inch pie shells, unbaked (see Tip)
1 egg, separated
½ cup apricot jam, heated
1 cup granulated sugar
8 ounces cream cheese, at room temperature
1 tablespoon cornstarch or arrowroot powder

1 can (14 ounce) apricot halves, drained (reserve ½ cup liquid)
½ cup dark brown sugar
1 tablespoon butter
½ cup slivered almonds, toasted

Preheat oven to 350 degrees.

Pierce bottoms of pie shells, brush with egg white, and bake for 15 to 20 minutes or until golden. Remove from oven and spread bottoms of pie shells with apricot jam. Set aside to cool.

Cream sugar and egg yolk together on high speed for five minutes or until light and lemon-yellow in color. Add cream cheese a little at a time and beat until smooth. Set aside.

To prepare topping, dilute cornstarch in 1 tablespoon water and add to reserved apricot liquid. Heat in a saucepan to boiling, whisking constantly until thickened. Add brown sugar and whisk until completely melted. Add butter and whisk until smooth.

Pour cream cheese mixture into pie shell. Place apricot halves around edges of pies. Cover apricots with sauce and sprinkle toasted almonds on top. Chill in refrigerator. Remove 30 minutes before serving.

Chef's tip: Pet-Ritz shortbread pie crust is an excellent, flaky crust.

Chef's tip: When baking the pie shell, check every five minutes and poke down any crust that puffs up. This can be done even after the shell is removed from the oven, but not after it has begun to cool. Air pockets under the crust will allow filling to seep under the crust and make it prematurely soggy.

Chef's tip: If apricots are canned in light syrup, heat and reduce to ½ cup. Filling will be too runny if liquid is not reduced.

Sugar Tree Inn

Luckily, Sugar Tree Inn sends maps with reservation confirmations. The inn seems utterly secluded from the rest of the world, yet is only six miles from an interstate. You are almost there when you reach Vesuvius, a sleepy little village with a general store and post office under one roof. On the steep three-mile climb up the mountain, take a few minutes to view the Shenandoah Valley rimmed with the majestic Blue Ridge Mountains. The road cuts through deep woods and passes bubbling brooks and waterfalls. After a final hairpin curve, the inn comes into view atop a 3,000-foot mountain.

Sugar Tree is a large rustic log cabin with inviting rocking chairs and a swing on the front porch. It is the perfect place to spend an afternoon gazing at magnificent vistas. The dogwoods were in full bloom during our tour. Springtime at Sugar Tree is special, but my thoughts wandered ahead to fall. How brilliant the sugar maples must be when the leaves turn!

The rooms in the main inn are quite pleasant, but my choice was a room in the guest house beneath the main inn and within walking distance of the dining room. My room had a large fireplace. The night of my stay, the temperature fell below freezing. The roaring fire and thick country quilts were necessities that evening.

Sugar Tree Inn, a labor of love, was built by local craftsmen over a period of six years, using pioneer techniques. No nails were used. Hand-hewn logs of oak, chestnut, and poplar, more than 125 years old, were notched and locked. The logs came from six cabins in the area. Carla Boddy, the young innkeeper, knows the history of each cabin and how it was used. The fireplace in the inn living room — which contains fifty-five tons of quarried limestone, all set by hand — is used throughout the inn's three seasons. In winter, Sugar Tree is closed because of impassable roads.

Dinner is served in a charming solarium built almost into the mountainside. The view from the table is the rising mountain, sprinkled with outdoor lighting.

A simple blackboard reveals the chef's specialties for the evening. My choice, Veal Arletta, was perhaps the tastiest veal I have eaten. The service was quick and quiet.

After a delightful dinner, the chef, Regina Clark, talked with us about her love of cooking. This is more than a job with her; it is something she lives and breathes.

At Sugar Tree, you can walk the trails, smell the flowers, and listen to the wood crackle in the fireplace. You can experience the Blue Ridge Mountains and the Shenandoah Valley all in one trip. Sugar Tree is an inn for romantics, a wonderful hideaway from a busy world.

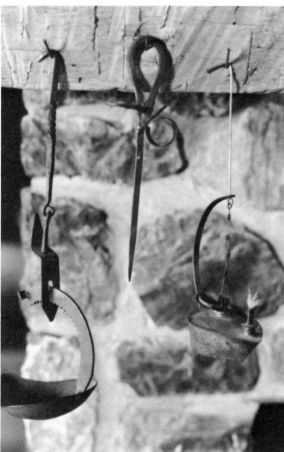

Sugar Tree Inn

Sugar Tree Inn
Vesuvius,
Virginia 24483
703-377-2197
Innkeepers:
Carla Boddy
The Schroeder Family

Orange and Cinnamon French Toast

Serves 6

1 loaf French bread
4 eggs
½ teaspoon pure orange extract
2 tablespoons orange juice
1 tablespoon cinnamon
   (enough to change color of
   eggs)

Garnish

Confectioners' sugar
Mandarin orange slices
   (optional)

Cut French bread in diagonal slices ½-inch thick, or thinner if desired. Whisk eggs with orange extract, orange juice, and cinnamon. Lightly butter griddle. Dip bread slices in egg mixture and cook on each side until golden brown. Arrange toast on platter, sprinkle with confectioners' sugar and top with mandarin orange sections if desired.

Chef's tip: Thinly sliced French bread will yield light and delicate toast. Cut bread thicker for more substantial toast.

Sugar Tree Inn

Veal Arletta

Serves 4

4 veal scallops
Flour
Butter
1 minced shallot
1 heart of palm, sliced in
    rounds
3 artichoke hearts (canned),
    cut in halves
1 tablespoon brandy
¼ cup heavy cream

Pound veal with a mallet until very tender and thin. Dredge veal in flour and sauté in hot butter on high heat. Remove veal from skillet to heated platter.

Sauté shallot, heart of palm, and artichoke hearts in skillet. Add brandy to pan. Avert your face and light with a match. When flames subside, add heavy cream. Return veal to skillet, and heat in sauce over moderate heat.

Tip: If you do not have heart of palm, substitute mushrooms, since they have the same texture.

Pecan Bread

Yields three 9-inch loaves

2 packages active dry yeast
1½ cups warm water
½ cup sugar
1 cup (2 sticks) butter
1 cup oil
1 cup milk
4 eggs
1 cup chopped pecans
7½ cups all-purpose flour
2 teaspoons salt

Preheat oven to 400 degrees.

Dissolve yeast in warm water, add sugar, and allow to stand about 10 minutes. In a separate pan, melt butter, add oil and milk, and heat until warm. Add to yeast mixture. Add eggs, pecans, flour, and salt, and beat well until all ingredients are combined and dough is sticky to the touch. Place in a greased bowl to rise. After dough rises, about 1 hour, punch down and let rise again, about 1 hour. Knead for about 10 minutes. Divide into three equal portions and shape into loaves. Let rise and bake for 25 minutes until tops are golden brown.

Chef's tip: Dough can be refrigerated overnight. Be sure to punch down one time after dough rises in refrigerator. Cover bowl with plastic wrap.

Tip: This is a dense, yeasty pecan bread. We liked it almost as well toasted and buttered the next morning as we did hot out of the oven the previous night.

Sugar Tree Inn

Banana Bourbon Cake

Serves 12

1½ cups chopped pecans
1½ cups golden raisins
3 cups all-purpose flour
3 teaspoons baking powder
1 teaspoon cinnamon
1 teaspoon ginger
½ teaspoon nutmeg
1 cup (2 sticks) unsalted
    butter, at room
    temperature
2 cups sugar
3 ripe bananas
4 eggs
¾ cup bourbon

Chef's tip: Sift flour three times before measuring for cake.

Preheat oven to 350 degrees.

Toss pecans and raisins with ½ cup flour. Set aside. Sift remaining 2½ cups flour with baking powder, cinnamon, ginger, and nutmeg. Set aside.

Beat butter and sugar until light and fluffy. Mash bananas into mixture. Add eggs one at a time, stirring after each one. Fold in flour mixture alternately with bourbon, beginning and ending with dry ingredients. Fold in pecans and raisins. Pour batter into ungreased 10-inch tube pan. Bake 1 hour or until done. Cool and remove from pan. Frost with Bourbon Icing.

Bourbon Icing

½ cup (1 stick) butter, at
    room temperature
1 package (8 ounce) cream
    cheese
1 pound confectioners' sugar
3 tablespoons bourbon or to
    taste

Tip: Be sure the cake is cool before icing.

Cream butter and cream cheese. Add confectioners' sugar and bourbon.

The Springs

An exhausted Indian brave, while running through the Allegheny Valley more than 200 years ago, came upon steaming hot water which had seeped through cracks and formed small pools. According to legend, the brave was rejuvenated by the exhilarating water.

These pools are now part of the Warm Springs Valley, which includes three springs: Warm Springs, Hot Springs, and Healing Springs. Rustic white pool houses are visible from U.S. Route 220. The men's bathhouse, built at Warm Springs in 1761, is said to be one of the oldest bath structures still in use. George Washington, Thomas Jefferson, and Robert E. Lee visited the bathhouse many times. The women's bathhouse was built in 1836. Locals told me that Mrs. Robert E. Lee used a separate area of the house, partitioned off from the main pool. A chair attached to a platform, used to lower her into the pool, is still there.

Before you leave the Warm Springs pool, drink a cup of the healing waters. No guarantees are made today, but you may walk away feeling just a little healthier!

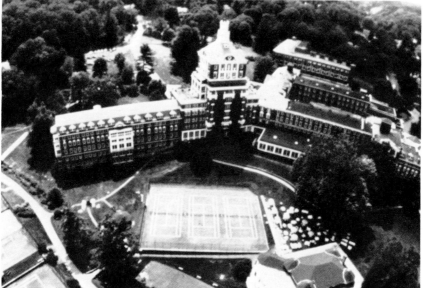

The Homestead

The Homestead is considered the grande dame of Virginia resorts. It is not an inn in the true sense of the word, but a historic hotel with 650 rooms which can accommodate 1,100 guests, in a magnificent setting of 15,000 acres of verdant countryside. The Homestead, grand in size, rises from the small village of Hot Springs against a dramatic backdrop of the Allegheny Mountains.

My first view of the Homestead was an unseasonably cold spring evening when the full moon seemed to spotlight the sprawling complex of buildings.

As I walked past rocker after rocker awaiting porch-sitters, into the great hall with its chandeliers and chintz wing chairs, I was amazed to see how the Homestead has survived the times.

"Society" orchestra music drifted from the main dining room. The musical selections were from another day, another time. As I was seated in the grand dining room I noticed how everything has been carefully preserved, including the murals, the boldly patterned carpet, and the shining hardwood dance floor. If I had closed my eyes, I am sure elegant couples from the 1930s would have appeared, dancing, right before my eyes. During those days, the elite of America, including Mrs. Cornelius Vanderbilt, summered at the Homestead, which was considered "the" social spa. Guests are still pampered, just as in the days when people traveled by train to this popular spa to enjoy the cool mountain breezes and take "the cure" at the springs.

The first Homestead was built in 1766 by Thomas Bullitt who, legend says, had received many requests for room and board in his own home.

More than 200 years later, the Homestead is a resort rich in tradition and offering many activities. Guests enjoy trapshooting, indoor bowling, swimming, fishing in wilderness streams, skiing, tennis, horseback riding, carriage rides, and much more. Golfing is a serious sport at the Homestead. The first tee, laid out in 1892, is the oldest in continuous use in the United States.

Executive Chef Albert Schnarwyler — who came from Lucerne, Switzerland, to the Homestead in 1962 — is in command of the massive food operation. From the enormous kitchens — virtually impossible to reproduce today — Chef Schnarwyler oversees approximately sixty-five cooks, bakers, and pastry chefs who prepare American and Continental dishes from his prized recipes.

One of the highlights of a day at the Homestead is afternoon tea, served promptly at 4 p.m. A string ensemble provides music while guests sip and visit in the great hall, in a tradition which has spanned generations. It is nice to know that time does not necessarily change everything. The Homestead is living proof.

The Homestead

Stuffed Sole Amoureuse

Serves 4

1½ pounds Boston sole fillets

4 ounces fresh spinach

1 tablespoon butter

1 teaspoon chopped shallots

¼ teaspoon salt

¼ teaspoon pepper

8 anise seeds

4 cups heavy cream

2 eggs

1 cup fish stock or diluted clam broth

1¼ cups white wine

1 live lobster, 1 to 1¼ pounds

2 tablespoons olive oil

2 teaspoons Pernod (licorice-flavored liqueur)

½ teaspoon chopped fresh tarragon, or ¼ teaspoon dried

½ teaspoon chopped fresh parsley

Tip: Preparation and cooking time for this recipe require about three hours, but the result is well worth the time and effort.

Tip: Use a live lobster for this recipe, if possible. You can have the butcher remove the tail, but preparation must then begin immediately. For testing purposes, I asked the butcher to barely steam the lobster (the shell had hardly started to change color). This also requires that the lobster be used immediately.

Chef's tip: The spinach can be squeezed dry and laid on top of the sole instead of processing the spinach and sole together. For this method, double the amount of spinach and spread the sole mousse on top of the spinach.

Preheat oven to 325 degrees.

Divide 1 pound of sole into two portions, reserving the remaining ½ pound. Flatten each portion between sheets of waxed paper. Overlap the fillets and form two large pieces, carefully pounding each with a mallet. Set aside.

Grind the reserved ½ pound of sole, and refrigerate. Cook spinach lightly in 2 teaspoons butter with ½ teaspoon shallots. Season with salt, pepper, and anise seeds. Cool, drain all liquid, and grind spinach. Mix the ground sole and spinach in a food processor with 1 cup of the cream, eggs, salt, and pepper. Blend well. Remove top sheet of waxed paper from flattened sole. Carefully spread spinach mousse on sole and roll up, removing bottom sheet of waxed paper as you roll. Repeat with second roll and set aside.

Butter a pan (usable on top of the stove as well as in the oven) with remaining butter, add fish stock, 1 cup white wine, and the fish rolls. Cover rolls with waxed paper. Add the tail section of the lobster. Bring to a simmer on top of stove, place in the preheated oven, and bake for 10 minutes. When done, remove fish rolls from liquid and keep warm, covered with waxed paper. Remove lobster tail and allow to cool. Remove lobster tail from shell and slice for garnish. On top of stove, reduce the liquid to 1 cup by simmering. Set aside.

Crush the body and claws of the lobster using a mallet or hammer. Sauté in hot olive oil over moderate heat until lobster shell turns red. Add chopped shallots, and sauté lightly before adding ¼ cup white wine, the reduced fish stock, Pernod, and 3 cups heavy cream. Strain through a double layer of cheesecloth. Return to heat and reduce to a light creamy sauce, yielding approximately 2 cups. Add chopped fresh tarragon and chopped parsley.

Slice sole approximately 1 inch thick. Spoon sauce over sole, garnish with lobster slices, and serve.

The Homestead

Fassifern Tomatoes

Serves 10

1 can (28 ounce) tomatoes
½ cup sugar
Salt and pepper to taste
·1 tablespoon cornstarch
2 cups toasted bread cubes
½ cup (1 stick) butter,
    melted

Preheat oven to 350 degrees.

Heat the tomatoes, sugar, salt, and pepper in a saucepan until hot. Mix the cornstarch with enough cold water to make a paste. Add to the hot mixture and simmer for 15 minutes. Place in a buttered baking dish (11½ x 7½ x 2-inch), uncovered, and put bread cubes on top. Cover with melted butter and bake for 30 minutes.

Virginia Pumpkin Pie

Yields two 10-inch pies

2 tablespoons butter
2 large cooking apples,
    peeled, cored, and cut in
    ¼-inch slices
1 teaspoon ground cinnamon
1 tablespoon granulated
    sugar
2 10-inch pie shells, unbaked

Filling

1 can (16 ounce) pumpkin
    purée
2 tablespoons molasses
½ teaspoon allspice
½ teaspoon ground
    cinnamon

¼ teaspoon ground ginger
2 cups (1 pint) light cream
    or half-and-half
5 eggs, beaten
1¼ cups sugar
Pinch salt

Preheat oven to 350 degrees.

Heat butter in skillet and lightly fry apples, cinnamon, and sugar. Cover the bottom of unbaked pie shell with apple mixture.

  Combine all filling ingredients, beat well, and pour over apple mixture. Bake for approximately 50 minutes or until done.

The Homestead
Hot Springs,
Virginia 24445
703-839-5500
800-336-5771
800-542-5734 (in
Virginia)

Chef's tip: The Homestead's recipes for "stewed" tomatoes is named for the "Fassifern Farms," a small Bath County, Virginia inn famous for its good food in the early 1900s.

Tip: This recipe is very good, but sweeter than most stewed-tomato recipes. Adjust sugar to your taste.

The Inn
at
Gristmill Square

The sun had just disappeared behind the mountains as we made the sharp turn off Highway 39 leading to the Inn at Gristmill Square, in the peaceful village of Warm Springs, Bath County seat. A welcome stillness surrounded the courthouse, antique shops, and inn complex. The babbling creek and a few crickets were the only noises in the cool spring air.

As early as 1761, people came to Warm Springs to take the baths and drink the "healing" water. They still come to the pools to relax.

The Inn at Gristmill Square is composed of several wooden buildings from the late nineteenth century, surrounding a neatly kept stone courtyard. The inn has small, cozy rooms with country quilts and antiques, and large suites with modern furnishings and decor. Fresh flowers and candles are everywhere.

You can have a delicious Continental breakfast — featuring freshly baked banana-nut bread — in your room or in the inn's Waterwheel Restaurant, part of the old 1771 gristmill.

Janice McWilliams and her son Bruce are the gracious hosts. Ask Bruce to show you the wine cellar, with bottles shelved among the wheels and gears of the old mill.

Dinner is a treat, especially if you like trout caught fresh in the morning and served that evening. The chefs at the Inn at Gristmill Square prepare this area favorite in a variety of ways — pan-fried with black walnuts, broiled with fresh herb butter, baked and stuffed, or smoked over hickory chips and served with sharp horseradish sauce. If you're not a trout enthusiast, there are many equally inviting house specialities.

For sports-minded guests, the Bath and Tennis Club is just across the street. Within driving distance you can fish, hunt, hike, ride horses, and play golf, and the historic Warm Springs pools are within walking distance.

When Janice McWilliams and Jack, her late husband, came to Virginia in 1981, after twenty years of owning a successful inn in Vermont, their expertise transformed the Inn at Gristmill Square into an unpretentious, comfortable inn where guests are treated like old friends. Janice and Bruce carry on the family tradition.

Inn at Gristmill Square

Chocolate Bourbon Pie
Serves 8

Crust

4 tablespoons butter
2 ounces unsweetened
   chocolate
2 eggs
¼ teaspoon salt
1 cup sugar
½ teaspoon vanilla
1 cup flour
½ cup chopped pecans

Filling

¼ cup cold water
½ cup bourbon
1 tablespoon unflavored
   gelatin
5 egg yolks
¾ cup sugar
1 cup whipping cream

Garnish

2 cups (1 pint) whipping
   cream, whipped
Chocolate shavings

Tip: This quantity of bourbon provides a distinctive flavor. You may want to adjust the amount to your taste.

Preheat oven to 350 degrees.

Melt butter and chocolate in a double boiler. Set aside to cool. Beat eggs and salt until light and foamy. Add sugar and vanilla to egg mixture, and beat until creamy. Stir in chocolate mixture. Fold in 1 cup flour and add pecans. Press mixture into the bottom of an ungreased 10-inch springform pan. Bake for 25 minutes, and cool.

Combine water and bourbon in the top of a double boiler, sprinkle gelatin on top, and allow to soften.

Beat egg yolks until thick and lemon colored. Add sugar.

Melt gelatin in double boiler. When dissolved, pour mixture into egg yolks, and beat briskly.

Whip cream, and fold into egg mixture. Pour into crust and refrigerate for 4 hours or until set. Top with whipped cream and chocolate shavings, and serve.

Inn at Gristmill Square

Bourbon Shrimp
Serves 4 to 5

Tip: This recipe can be used as an appetizer or as an entrée.

3 tablespoons butter
1 pound shrimp (21 to 25
count), peeled and
deveined
¼ cup bourbon, or to taste
¼ cup heavy cream
¼ teaspoon salt, or to taste

Melt butter in a skillet. Add shrimp and sauté until pink and firm. (Do not overcook.) Splash shrimp with bourbon and remove to serving dish and keep warm. Add cream to skillet, scraping the bottom of the pan with a spatula as you do, and add salt. Heat the mixture over medium heat and pour over shrimp. Serve immediately.

Massillon Potatoes
Serves 2

Chef's tip: Potatoes must be large baking potatoes or aged potatoes with little water content.

1 large Idaho baking potato
Vegetable oil for deep frying

Slice potatoes as thinly as possible on a vegetable slicer or in a food processor. Place slices in cold water in refrigerator for 1 to 2 hours. Change water once.

Preheat oil to 375 degrees in a deep fryer or heavy pan. Drain potato slices and pat as dry as possible on a towel. Drop potatoes a handful at a time into the hot oil. Stir once or twice with a wooden spoon, cooking until golden brown (just a few seconds). Some potatoes will be crisp like hot potato chips; some will be softer in the middle. Drain on paper towels, salt, and serve immediately.

Chef's tip: Be sure to let the oil come back up to 375 degrees before adding each new batch of slices.

Inn at Gristmill Square

The Inn at
Gristmill Square
P.O. Box 359
Warm Springs,
Virginia 24484
703-839-2231
Innkeepers: Janice
McWilliams and Bruce
McWilliams

Waterwheel Restaurant
Baked Stuffed Trout

Serves 4

4 freshwater trout, 8 to 10
  ounces, filleted
2 tablespoons butter
1 small carrot, sliced into
  julienne strips
1 small zucchini, sliced into
  julienne strips
1 small to medium onion,
  sliced into strips
4 large mushrooms, sliced
  into julienne strips
½ teaspoon tarragon
½ teaspoon finely chopped
  parsley
¼ teaspoon each salt and
  pepper, or to taste
4 to 8 teaspoons white wine
4 sheets parchment paper or
  foil
4 lemon wedges

Preheat oven to 400 degrees.

Melt butter in a skillet and sauté vegetables. Season with
tarragon, parsley, salt and pepper. Cook until vegetables
begin to lose their crispness.

Divide vegetables into 4 portions and place on top of 4
halves of trout. Cover (sandwich style) with remaining 4
halves of trout (skin side up).

Place each stuffed trout on a piece of parchment paper
or foil. Fold like an envelope, leaving a small hole at the
top. Splash 1 to 2 teaspoons of white wine into each hole
and place trout on a baking sheet. Bake for 10 to 15 minutes or until trout is firm.

Remove paper or foil and serve with a wedge of lemon.

Martha Washington Inn

On the Fourth of July, American flags were waving in the air on Main Street as I arrived in Abingdon, Virginia. What better way to celebrate this national holiday than to observe the small-town festivities from the colonnaded veranda of the historic Martha Washington Inn?

Built in 1832 as a residence of Colonel Francis Preston and his wife, Sarah — Patrick Henry's niece — in 1858 it became Martha Washington College, a women's school which operated throughout the Civil War. It also doubled as a hospital for Union and Confederate soldiers.

Many conflicting ghost stories survive from the Civil War period. One tells of a seriously wounded Yankee boy nursed by a "Martha" girl who played her violin each evening to help ease his pain. His death broke her heart and, according to reports, distant strains of violin music can be heard in the hallways of the mansion from time to time. Ask about the ghost violinist and you may hear another version of the story.

In 1932 the college closed and the property reopened as a hotel, changing hands many times over the years. The present owner has spent millions of dollars restoring the inn with period antiques. From the impressive foyer with the magnificent staircase to the third-floor suites, careful attention has been given to the smallest details. The parlors opening off the spacious lobby have floors of burnished wood, and lace-draped, floor-to-ceiling windows from which you can see the Barter Theater, America's longest-running professional playhouse.

The Martha Washington Inn, with its superb accommodations and first-class dining room, is worth a trip to this scenic town. As I observed the beautifully restored homes and wandered in and out of the unique shops on Abingdon's historical walking tour, I was glad this particular stop was on my tour.

Martha Washington Inn

Martha Washington
Inn
150 West Main Street
Abingdon,
Virginia 24210
703-628-3161
800-533-1014 (in
Virginia)

Butternut Squash and Apple Soup

Serves 8

1 medium turnip, peeled and
    chopped
1 medium potato, peeled and
    chopped
1 pound butternut squash,
    peeled and chopped
1 large carrot, chopped
    (unpeeled)
1 medium onion, chopped
2 stalks celery, strings
    removed, chopped
2 Granny Smith apples,
    peeled, cored, and
    chopped
5 to 6 cups rich homemade
    chicken stock
2 cups (1 pint) heavy cream
½ cup natural apple juice

Boil turnip and potato together until tender. Drain and set
aside. Boil all remaining vegetables and apples in chicken
stock until tender, drain, and reserve liquid. Purée vegetables, including turnip and potato, in food processor or
blender, adding cream slowly. Recombine with stock, and
whisk. Add apple juice and whisk again. Serve
immediately.

Chef's tip: Use your
favorite homemade
chicken stock or canned
chicken broth.

Chef's tip: Use carrots
to test for tenderness,
since they require the
longest cooking time.

Martha Washington Inn

Stuffed Zucchini

Serves 4

4 tablespoons tomato sauce
½ teaspoon minced fresh dill
1 large zucchini squash
1 cup ricotta cheese mixture
2 slices (1 ounce each)
   mozzarella cheese

Ricotta Cheese Filling

½ cup (4 ounces) ricotta
   cheese
1 tablespoon grated
   Parmesan cheese
3 tablespoons shredded
   mozzarella cheese

⅛ teaspoon oregano
⅛ teaspoon basil
⅛ teaspoon marjoram
1 egg, beaten
⅛ teaspoon each salt and
   pepper, or to taste

Preheat oven to 350 degrees.

Combine tomato sauce, and dill, and let sit at least 20 minutes. Combine ingredients for filling, and set aside. Cut zucchini in half lengthwise, then cut in half crosswise. Scoop out pulp with melon-baller. Fill each quarter with ricotta cheese filling. Top each with half a slice of mozzarella cheese. Bake for 25 minutes. Top each quarter with 1 tablespoon tomato sauce, and serve.

Tip: The zucchini was cooked but still crisp after a baking time of 25 minutes. If you prefer more tender zucchini, increase the cooking time.

Martha Washington Inn

Spinach Soufflé

Serves 6 to 8

1 tablespoon butter
3 tablespoons grated
   Parmesan cheese
3 tablespoons flour
1 pound fresh spinach, or 1
   10-ounce package frozen
   spinach

Béchamel Sauce

4 tablespoons butter
4 tablespoons flour
1 cup milk
Salt and pepper to taste
⅛ teaspoon nutmeg
6 eggs, separated
Pinch of salt, for beating
   with egg whites

Butter soufflé dish (1½ quart or 6½-inch diameter) and refrigerate for 15 minutes. Mix the Parmesan cheese and flour. Take dish out of refrigerator and apply another coating of butter. Then sprinkle with cheese-and-flour mixture. Shake out excess.

Cook spinach in boiling salted water until just tender. Drain and place in bowl with cold water and ice cubes for 2 minutes. Drain again. Press out all moisture with paper towels.

In heavy saucepan, melt butter. Whisk in flour. Cook for about 5 minutes over medium heat, stirring constantly. In another saucepan, bring milk to boil. Whisk milk into butter-and-flour mixture until white sauce is thick and smooth. Season with salt, pepper, and nutmeg. Chop spinach in food processor with steel blade, or purée in blender. Add white sauce to blender, and mix. Add 3 egg yolks to blender and blend for 5 seconds at high speed. Add the remaining 3 yolks and repeat. Transfer mixture to a large mixing bowl.

With electric mixer, beat the egg whites with a pinch of salt until soft peaks form. Fold one-third of egg whites into spinach mixture. Fold in remaining egg whites quickly with a rubber spatula. Pour into prepared soufflé dish and set on baking sheet. Bake for 30 to 35 minutes or until firm. Serve immediately.

Martha Washington Inn

Chicken Parmesan

Serves 4

4 chicken breasts (8 ounces
   each), skinned and boned
1 cup seasoned bread crumbs
½ cup grated fresh Parmesan
   cheese
4 tablespoons olive oil, or
   more if necessary

2 tablespoons tomato paste
6 fresh basil leaves, chopped
¼ cup good red wine
   (Burgundy or Bordeaux)
2 medium tomatoes, peeled,
   seeded, and chopped

Tip: To peel tomatoes, place them in a pan of boiling water for 40 seconds. Drain hot water and dip tomatoes in cool tap water. Skins will crack and slip off easily.

Coat chicken breasts with a mixture of the bread crumbs and Parmesan cheese. Heat olive oil in a sauté pan over medium heat. Brown breasts on both sides. When cooked, remove breasts from pan and keep warm. Add tomato paste and basil to sauté pan and cook for about 2 minutes. Deglaze pan by adding red wine and scraping bottom of pan as wine comes to a boil. Cook until liquid is reduced by one-third. Add fresh tomatoes and cook for 3 minutes. Top chicken with sauce and serve immediately.

Martha Washington Inn

Sea Scallops
with Orange and Saffron

Serves 4

1 pound fresh sea scallops
  (16 to 20 per pound)
1 orange
1 tomato, skinned, seeded,
  and diced
½ teaspoon saffron threads

Salt and pepper to taste
½ teaspoon butter
1 small shallot, finely
  chopped
2 tablespoons dry white
  wine
¼ cup heavy cream

Garnish

2 tablespoons chopped fresh
  parsley
4 orange wheels, split and
  twisted

Thoroughly wash any grit from scallops, and drain. Slice each scallop into thirds or ¼-inch thick and set aside.

Grate the rind of 1 orange and squeeze the juice into a bowl. Add grated rind, tomato, saffron, salt, and pepper to the juice to prepare marinade. Place scallops in marinade, cover, and refrigerate for four hours or longer.

Melt butter in sauté pan, add shallots, and turn heat to high. With a slotted spoon, remove scallops from marinade (reserve marinade) and add to butter in sauté pan. Cook scallops for 1 minute over high heat. Do not overcook. Remove scallops to heated serving dish.

Add white wine, reserved marinade, and heavy cream to pan. Cook over medium heat, and stir until reduced by half. Return scallops to pan and bring to boil. Remove from heat. Serve sprinkled with parsley and twisted orange peels.

Chef's tip: Do not include any of the white pith when grating the orange rind; it will be bitter.

Chef's tip: Stir scallops occasionally with a rubber spatula instead of a metal spoon, to prevent slices from breaking.

Martha Washington Inn

Peach Cheesecake

Crust

2 cups graham cracker
  crumbs
½ cup (1 stick) butter,
  melted
¼ cup brown sugar
¼ cup grated white chocolate
  (optional)

Cheese Filling

4 packages (8 ounces each)
  cream cheese, softened
1½ cups granulated sugar
1 envelope unflavored gelatin
¼ cup peach schnapps
1 teaspoon real vanilla
  extract
¼ cup puréed peaches
4 eggs

Sour Cream Topping

2 cups (16 ounces) sour
  cream
½ cup granulated sugar
⅛ teaspoon real vanilla
  extract
1 tablespoon orange, lemon,
  or other extract

Preheat oven to 350 degrees.

Combine crust ingredients and press into the bottom of a 9-inch springform pan.

Beat cream cheese and sugar until light and creamy. Add gelatin, schnapps, vanilla, and puréed peaches. Remove from mixer and blend in eggs, 2 at a time, by hand. Pour cheese filling into pan and bake for 50 minutes. Cool on rack for 10 minutes.

Combine topping ingredients. Mix at medium speed for 30 seconds, then at high speed for 1 minute. Spread topping over cake after it has cooled for 10 minutes. Return to oven for 10 minutes. Put directly from oven to refrigerator (leave on rack) to cool for 4 to 5 hours.

Chef's tip: Use one fresh peach, peeled and pitted, or two canned peach halves, well drained, for purée.

Chef's tip: Do not use an electric mixer when adding the eggs.

Chef's tip: Removing the cake from the oven to cool for 10 minutes, spreading the topping, and baking for another 10 minutes will reduce the likelihood that the cake will crack when the springform pan is removed.

Index

Acknowledgements

Florentine cover paper and inside cover border reprinted with permission
from Cartotechnica A. Ross s.a.s., Florence, Italy,
copyright holder.

Food consultant,
Ellen Fly
Editing,
Hazel Rowena Mills
Chromatecs Dry Transfers,
Statworks
Photo processing,
Prints Unlimited

This book was printed on 70 lb. Patina matte with 80 lb. Patina matte
plus lamination for cover over 120-point binder's board
by Wimmer Brothers, Inc. in Memphis & Dallas.

"Chef's Tips" and "Tips"

Many of the recipes appearing in this book are usually prepared in large quantities or in the convenience of professionally staffed kitchens. To assist the reader, I asked the chefs to provide helpful tips for preparing their recipes — these are "Chef's tips." The other recipe testers and I also took careful note of any information we thought might be beneficial to the reader — these are included as "Tips." I hope they are of assistance and will add to your cooking pleasure.

The Inns

Special thanks to the innkeepers and chefs who shared their recipes and answered our many questions during the testing of the recipes. The inns which appear in this book did not pay to be included. They contributed valuable time, information, and recipes.
    Grateful acknowledgement is made to the following:
The Red Fox Tavern, Middleburg, Virginia: photo, pages 43-44. The Boar's Head Inn, Charlottesville, Virginia: photo, pages 100-101. The Homestead Inn, Hot Springs, Virginia: aerial photo, page 130. *Thomas Jefferson's Cookbook* by Marie Kimbell, published by The University Press of Virginia: recipes, pages 10, 11, 103. *The Williamsburg Cookbook*, published by The Colonial Williamsburg Foundation: recipe, page 21.

Our appreciation for their assistance to Simon David Foods and Marty's, both of Dallas, Texas.

M'Layne Murphy